The Italian Commonwealth

Significant Issues Series
Timely books presenting current CSIS research and analysis of interest to
the academic, business, government, and policy communities.
Managing Editor: Roberta L. Howard

The Center for Strategic and International Studies (CSIS), established in
1962, is a private, tax-exempt institution focusing on international public
policy issues. Its research is nonpartisan and nonproprietary.

CSIS is dedicated to policy analysis and impact. It seeks to inform and
shape selected policy decisions in government and the private sector to meet
the increasingly complex and difficult global challenges that leaders will
confront in the next century. It achieves this mission in three ways: by
generating strategic analysis that is anticipatory and interdisciplinary; by
convening policymakers and other influential parties to assess key issues;
and by building structures for policy action.

CSIS does not take specific public policy positions. Accordingly, all
views, positions, and conclusions expressed in this publication should be
understood to be solely those of the authors.

The CSIS Press
1800 K Street, N.W., Washington, D.C. 20006
Telephone: (202) 887-0200 Fax: (202) 775-3199
E-mail: books@csis.org Web site: http://www.csis.org/

This volume in the Significant Issues Series is produced by CSIS's New Italy
Project in cooperation with *liMes, Rivista Italiana di Geopolitica.*

liMes, Rivista Italiana di Geopolitica
viale del Castro Pretorio 116 - 00185 Rome, Italy
Telephone: 39-6-4940432 Fax: 39-6-4940403
E-mail: logoi@starfarm.it
Web site: http://www.starfarm.it/logoi/

CSIS New Italy Project
Telephone: (202) 775-3284; (202) 775-3216
Fax: (202) 775-3199 E-mail: Emaffia@csis.org

The Italian Commonwealth

liMes

THE CSIS PRESS
CENTER FOR STRATEGIC & INTERNATIONAL STUDIES
Washington, D.C.

Significant Issues Series, Volume XXI, Number 4
© 1999 by the Center for Strategic and International Studies
Washington, D.C. 20006
Printed on recycled paper in the United States of America

01   00   99   3   2   1

ISSN 0736-7136
ISBN 0-89206-354-8

Cover design by Meadows Design Office
Printing by Reproductions, Inc.

Library of Congress Cataloging-in-Publication Data
The Italian commonwealth / liMes ;
         p.   cm. — (Significant issues series , ISSN 0736–7136   ;
v. 21, no. 4)
      "liMes."
      Includes bibliographical references.
      ISBN 0-89206-354-8 (alk. paper)
      1. Italy—Politics and government—1994– 2. Italy—Foreign
relations—1994– 3. Italy—Economic conditions—1994– .
I. Limes. Special number.   II. Series.
      DG583.5.I75   1999
      712'.6'0945—dc21   99-30824
                                                CIP

Contents

Contributors   vii

Introduction   ix

1
In Search of the Italian Diaspora   1
Andrea Bianchi

2
How Italian Is the Universal Church?   11
Stefano Picciaredda

3
**Pacific Calling Mediterranean:
A Future for Our Ports   24**
Adalberto Vallega

4
A User's Manual for Italy   41
Alfonso Desiderio

5
**From "Made in Italy" to *Sistema Italia:*
In Search of an Internationalization Strategy   57**
Marta Dassù and Roberto Menotti

Contributors

ANDREA BIANCHI—Journalist, *Gazzettino*

MARTA DASSÙ—Director, CESPI (Center for International Political Studies)

ALFONSO DESIDERIO—Journalist, international affairs expert

ROBERTO MENOTTI—Researcher, CESPI (Center for International Political Studies)

STEFANO PICCIAREDDA—Researcher

ADALBERTO VALLEGA—Geographer, professor at University of Genoa

Introduction

Almost every major European nation has its own overseas network. Great Britain has the Commonwealth, France promotes a Francophone community of nations, Spain the *hispanidad* that reverberates in Iberian-American summits; even Portugal plays the card of Lusophony. Two mysterious cases remain, however: Germany and Italy. The first is not so enigmatic, as Germans, because of their past, cannot mobilize their considerable ethnic potential in the United States or elsewhere without raising suspicions of hegemonic aims. The second case is more obscure. Why has Italy, which can count on a real diaspora (almost 60 million people of Italian extraction in the world by some estimates), and certainly does not scare anyone, never mobilized this force to defend its own national interests? Perhaps such a hands-off approach was understandable during the Cold War, when Italians were "cuddled" by the Americans; but now, in the famous era of globalization, this reticence is not justified.

Certainly, it is known that the image of Italy spread by Italian immigrants corresponds more often to the memory of the village their grandparents left behind than to the reality of today's Italy. It is also clear that the Italian state cannot assume the responsibility to invent a global Italian network on its own. It is mainly the Italians, in Italian society and in the world, who should create the conditions for an international Italian community.

On the other hand, the Italian diaspora is not the only element that could be deployed to Italy's advantage. In this volume we examine various sources of power that Italy can draw from on a global scale: the vitality of small and medium-sized enterprise and the model of industrial districts; the increasing presence of Italian regions and local entities in the international arena (as long as it is consistent with the national interest); the Roman Catholic

Church, ecumenical yet still strongly "Italian"; an artistic patri-mony without equal; a successful "Italian lifestyle" (fashion, de-sign, sport, cooking, music). All these phenomena and factors can be deployed in random order, as has been done so far, or, in-stead, put in a network to defend the prestige, the rank, and in-terests of the country.

The Italian community (or whatever it will be called) would be above all a useful tool to prevent Italy from becoming a mar-ginal player in Europe. Playing in Europe with only European weapons means to condemn Italy to lose. To count in Europe we need to act on all levels, the global one included. This is why *li*Mes wants to initiate a geopolitical debate that will go beyond this volume and that will try to foster a discussion on the charac-teristics, the role, and the organization of the Italian community in the world.

1

In Search of the Italian Diaspora

Andrea Bianchi

Rome may be discovering the importance of the approximately 60 million men and women of Italian descent worldwide. . . . Census problems. . . . Existing and potential lobbies. . . . A strategic presence in the United States and Australia.

Italy's list of missed opportunities has never been a short one, but the Italians living abroad easily rank at the top of it. Italy has been unable to awaken the millions of citizens and, especially, tens of millions of men and women of Italian descent into a force to be reckoned with in world affairs. They could almost be called a "dormant commonwealth," potentially at the service of Italian geopolitics, if there were such a thing. They would be an even more valuable asset in the near future, when the process of European integration inevitably reins in the scant freedom Italy still has to act independently on the world stage, as it becomes more and more part of the European Union and less and less an independent player.

Italian Citizens: How Many and Where?

A reliable census of Italian citizens abroad is the essential condition of any serious policy to deal with them. Italian citizens residing abroad maintain close ties to home and are naturally the country's foremost ambassadors. Unfortunately, at least in theory the legislative tools needed to create a registry of Italians abroad have been around for only a few years.

Law 470/1988, with the title "Registry and Census of Italians Abroad," came about in connection with the Second National Conference on Emigration, held in Rome from November 28 to December 3, 1988. The conference closed with a call for a series of political and administrative initiatives to aid the Italian community abroad. As recently as 30 years ago, a person moving to another country was taken off the books of his or her municipality of residence, and so "disappeared." Emigrants' records were later kept on file at city hall. For the purposes of law 470/1988, these records currently constitute the bulk of the Registry of Italians Living Abroad (AIRE) kept at the Ministry of the Interior, while the so-called special section houses data on Italian citizens born and living abroad whose ancestors were not born in Italy and never lived there.

The law also called for a "survey" of Italian citizens living abroad as permanent residents or for less than 12 months, in parallel with the general census of citizens residing within Italy, assigning the task to the consular offices.

Foreseeably, the effort kicked-off with the 1991 general census was largely unsuccessful, due to the practical impossibility of identifying and contacting a reasonable number of citizens residing abroad and getting them to fill out the forms from the Italian Central Bureau of Statistics (ISTAT). Thus, the official starting point remains AIRE, which includes data on individuals who reobtained Italian citizenship pursuant to law 91/1992 and other information.

Law 91/1992, which introduced dual citizenship and entered into force on August 15, 1992, set a deadline for applying to reobtain citizenship, which was extended several times to December 31, 1997. It is still too early to judge, but the law seems to have had a limited impact: approximately 40,000 lapsed citizenships were renewed in 1992-94, a small number in relation to the potential pool. Based on data from January 2, 1998, AIRE has records on 2,497,968 citizens in all, with 1,459,652 in Europe, 417,566 in North and Central America, 368,266 in South America, and 118,960 in Oceania.

The Interior Ministry figures do not agree with data gathered by another government agency, the Ministry of Foreign Affairs. Since 1968 it has been generating annual estimates of the size of Italian communities abroad. Ten years ago it published a summary of that work in anticipation of the conference on emigration.[1] At that time the figures were approximately 5,124,000 Italian citizens abroad, with some 2,250,000 in the Americas and 2,192,000 in Europe. Subsequent data gathering has adjusted those figures sharply downward. As of December 22, 1997, the so-called consular registry counted 3,473,018 citizens in all, with 1,967,863 in Europe, 307,361 in North and Central America, and 1,021,960 in South America.

The roughly million-individual discrepancy with respect to the AIRE figure can be explained by a number of factors. Voluntary registration within consular immigration districts is often difficult due to the size of the district, which can be as large as an entire state, and it is certainly not made any easier by the cutback in diplomatic offices. Questions can also be raised about how accurately individuals are removed from one list when they move to another district, which would overstate the number of Italians in the consular registry. On the other hand, AIRE almost certainly does not have records on all Italian citizens residing abroad. The law establishing it is not very well publicized, so the people to whom it is directed are not inclined to take action. There is also an important subjective factor that should not be discounted: registering with AIRE means "showing up on the radar screen" of the Italian bureaucracy, with all that entails. For example, it means disclosing one's whereabouts to the internal revenue authorities or the selective service administration. These disadvantages are not always offset by any advantages to be gained by registering, such as access to welfare benefits and public assistance.

People of Italian Descent: How Many and Where?

A census of the world population of Italian descent is a very difficult thing to attempt, and perhaps flies in the face of common sense to some extent. We hear big numbers—up to 50 or 60 million individuals descended from Italian emigrants—and they are supported by the migratory outflows from Italy over the past century. Approximately 26.6 million Italians left their country between 1876 and 1987: 12.5 million for non-European countries (mainly the Americas and Australia) with 14.1 million settling in Europe. According to ISTAT data, emigration reached its peak in the decade 1901-1910 (more than 6 million) and remained strong throughout the decade that followed (3.8 million). Emigration was a mass phenomenon even after the Second World War. In all, more than 5.6 million Italians left their country between 1951 and 1970. Some 50,000 to 60,000 people have dropped off the public registries to move abroad every year since 1987—a "physiological rate."

Today, Italy is more a destination than point of embarkation for emigrants. In theory, therefore, the high current figures thrown about in the press could be viewed as unreliable, at least from the mathematical standpoint. The Foreign Ministry publication referenced above estimated the number of second-, third-, and fourth-generation Italians worldwide at 58.5 million in 1987, with 39.8 million in South America, 16 million in North America, 1.9 million in Europe, and one-half million in Oceania. But an accurate check can be made in only a few instances, where the host countries' bureaus of statistics include ethnic origin, or at least the language spoken in the home, on their questionnaires.

Of the five major destinations for Italian emigration—the United States, Canada, Australia, Argentina, and Brazil—only the first three can be double-checked. Since 1980 the U.S. Bureau of the Census has asked American citizens to state their ethnic origin. But the question allows for multiple responses influenced by objective factors (such as the parents' native country) and subjective factors. Because the interviewee can choose to leave the question blank or select the generic response "American," stating a specific origin is clearly a sign that the respondent feels at least a superficial kinship with the native group. This is a crucial point, as it would be a mistake to develop a geopolitical argument based on any number without asking the real question: How much of a sense of belonging can these people still feel for their ancestors' native country, or how receptive to it can they be?

The 1990 census identified about 15 million Americans as "Italian American," ranking fifth behind German, English, Irish, and African American. The same Bureau of the Census, however, estimates that today one American in 10 has Italian blood running in his or her veins, which would boost the number to about 25 million. Italian Americans are mainly concentrated on the eastern seaboard, with four states topping one million: New York (2.9 million), New Jersey (1.5 million), Pennsylvania (1.4 million), and, on the West Coast, California (1.5 million).

The surveys conducted by Statistics Canada are also very thorough. According to the 1991 census, there are 750,055 Canadians of Italian origin out of a total population of 26,994,045. The overwhelming majority of Italian Canadians live in the "historic" territories of Ontario (486,765) and Quebec (174,530).

A different but equally useful approach is employed by the Australian Bureau of Statistics, which has been asking for the "language spoken in the home" by Australian citizens for more than five years. In 1996 the Italian-language community, so-defined, numbered 367,290 out of a total population of 16,624,517.

The size of the population of Italian origin is harder to calculate for Brazil and Argentina, precisely the part of the world that had the greatest influx of Italian immigrants in the second half of the nineteenth and first half of the twentieth century. Statisticians measure factors other than national "roots," such as race, skin color, and religion, so we are working with estimates. The Foreign Ministry's 10-year-old statistics seem overstated when they claim 22.7 million people of Italian descent in Brazil and 15.5 in Argentina. The Brazil figure in particular arouses suspicion, given that the Agnelli Foundation, a staunch backer of studies in this area, counts 8 and 15 million citizens of Italian origin, respectively.[2] Even these could be "generous" figures, although it is true that there were 488,000 Italians in Argentina in 1980 out of a total of 1,903,000 foreign residents.[3] The initiatives launched by the Italians Abroad Department (Dipartimento Italiani nel Mondo) of the Italian Prime Minister's Office to survey the actual size of the worldwide Italian community through associations of Italians abroad have not met with success yet. A new effort is under way, however, the results of which will become available in a few months.

The "Dormant Commonwealth"

The problem of the relationship between Italy and Italians abroad is by definition a complicated one. American sociologist Joel Kotkin points out an interesting aspect of the problem when he observes that Italians do not behave like other large "tribes" contemporary with them (he cites the Jews, British, Japanese, Chinese, and Indians): they do not "develop their economic power within their own ethnic network."[4] Kotkin argues that the decisive factors in the success of "global tribes" are a very strong sense of ethnic identity, mutual trust that extends beyond national boundaries, and a passion for technological development. This hypothesis and the choice of which groups constitute the model "global tribes" could be argued back and forth at length, but—clearly—important cohesive factors like race, religion, and national feeling are lacking or have little impact among Italian communities. To get an idea of what Italians are missing out on, consider one of the best organized "minorities," world Jewry.

The Italian diaspora can be likened to the aftereffects of a national "big bang," with fragments getting further and further away from the center of the explosion and one another as they flew apart. The forces that could have held them together were, and still are, fairly weak, so the effects of integration into the host society have inevitably tended to dominate.

While Italians around the world join associations in great numbers—circles, charitable institutions, cooperatives, and so forth—a structured lobby of people of Italian descent active in a given sector of civic life seems fairly rare. The oft-cited example of the National Italian American Foundation (NIAF) is controversial in the United States as well, but would appear to be the exception to the rule. The flip side of the integration, social dynamism, and success experienced in countries where the emigrants had arrived without a dime (or a lira), but with high hopes, could be the survival among Italian immigrants of a picture of Italy as it once was, perhaps many years or decades ago. This will be less and less so as we move into the age of the Internet, but, if Hollywood is any indication, stereotypes of Italian Americans are alive and well, feeding on the expectations of an audience brought up on the many famous actors and directors of Italian descent.

Even so, the Italian diaspora's strong points should not be overlooked, first and foremost its geographical distribution in areas of great geopolitical interest, ranging from the heart of the "American Empire" to large developing countries, like Argentina or Brazil, to Australia, the "southern front" of Asian expansion. Italians' propensity for joining associations was alluded to earlier; the directory of associations of Italians around the world compiled by the Ministry of Foreign Affairs is a thick volume with close to 500 pages of names and addresses of thousands of organizations founded for an incredible variety of purposes, including public service, recreation, education, and facility management. Thus, there is a network of "contacts" to cultivate and develop. Easier still, as happens often in newspapers and on television, is to hold up as an example those individuals of Italian descent who have achieved success and power in their adoptive countries.

Examples from the business world are usually cited, and the list would be a very long one. But the world of politics also offers many examples, such as the 30 "Italian" members of the United States Congress, former New York governor Mario Cuomo, President Julio María Sanguinetti of Uruguay, Canadian Minister of International Trade Sergio Marchi and Minister of Public Works and Government Services Alfonso Gagliano, former Sydney mayor Frank Sartor, former deputy prime minister Elio Di Rupo of Belgium, and the special case of Sonia Maino-Gandhi, the heiress to the Gandhi dynasty who has been at the wheel of India's Congress Party since its inception.

Maybe it begs the question to say that a foreign politician of Italian descent is favorably disposed toward Italy, and maybe not. But it would be a shame not to find out. A politician stepping in on behalf of Italy is not without precedent. New York's legendary mayor Fiorello La Guardia came to Italian premier Alcide De Gasperi's aid right after the Second World War, when millions of Italians were in danger of starvation after grain stores ran out. More recently, in 1975, Italian Americans pressured President Gerald Ford not to exclude Italy from the Rambouillet Summit, at which the Group of Seven was to be founded. These are isolated events, as unlike other governments Italy does not usually make use of such channels. It is fair to criticize the NIAF's failure to lobby energetically, and to point out that it does little more than offer a number of scholarships and host the famed annual dinner attended by the president of the United States. But NIAF President Kenneth Ciongoli's 1996 statement raises doubts and is indicative of a way of doing things: "I am the president of an association that has been around for 20 years and represents thousands of Italian Americans, and I have been somewhat successful. Yet I have never been contacted on a regular basis by the cultural arms of the [Italian] government."[5]

Good Intentions

No one in Italy has any doubt that Italians living abroad—by which they mean generically both communities of citizens and people of Italian descent—represent a "resource" for the country. This maxim is trotted out as needed by representatives of all administrations, especially if the audience is highly sensitive to the issue. Just recently, in fact, while announcing the Third National Conference on Emigration for late 1998 or early 1999, Deputy Minister of Foreign Affairs Piero Fassino referred to the communities of fellow Italians abroad as "leverage for the Italian presence around the world" and explained that the executive branch had plans to "forge a link between the political choices made by Italy" and Italians abroad.[6] While this statement does herald a change, it also contains an admission (though not a hard one to make) that the resource represented by "Italians abroad" has gone substantially unutilized. The effort by the administration and the majority that supports it is directed mainly at citizens residing outside Italy.

Fassino predicted that the reform of the system of representation for Italians living abroad—ranging from the Commissions for Italians Abroad (COMITES) to the General Council on Italians Abroad (CGIE)—should come to fruition first in 1998. Such reform is deemed necessary, even though the acts establishing these bodies are new. The changes to be introduced by Italy's Parliament chiefly relate to establishing the COMITES elected by Italian citizens, and to some extent by foreign citizens, as "direct representatives" and "official points of contact" for the consular authorities. The bill that stands to resolve the age-old controversy of expatriate suffrage is also making headway in Parliament. However, the record of the past few legislatures, the sensitivity of the subject, and the timing concurrent with the constitutional reform bode especially ill for this initiative, which has always been at the top of Italian communities' wish lists.

The most important goal articulated by the deputy minister, though, is to hold the Third National Conference on Emigration, the first time the conference will be held in 10 years. Fassino sought to emphasize the different approach the administration wants to take to the Third Conference. Previously, the conference focused "mainly on the historical and social aspects" of the phenomenon of emigration. This time the focus will be on "the contribution that Italians and those descended from Italians who settled abroad have made to the development of the countries in which they live." Thus, the Third Conference "will showcase, in a sense, what Italians are today." In addition to representatives of Italian communities, the invitees will include "a few hundred notables who have achieved excellence in the fields of economics, science, and culture, and are most symbolic of the enormous contribution Italians have made to civilization and progress."

If anything comes of this, a conference open to the worldwide Italian elite could help identify the weaknesses and missed opportunities that have kept a wealth of goodwill toward Italy from being used "geopolitically" until now, and that wealth is certainly substantial. The terms "propaganda" and "lobby" have negative connotations to Italian ears: one has faint totalitarian overtones and the other evokes backroom scheming that "never took place." In fact, the best of governments enlist cultural institutes, foundations, and various kinds of organizations as a matter of course to supplement official diplomacy and enhance their country's image. Seen from that vantage point, Italy's efforts still leave much to be desired. As the recurring controversies over Italian cultural institutes indicate, the oft-cited shortcomings of these efforts include the failure to capture the interest of at least some of the vast number of people worldwide who feel some fondness for Italy, even if nothing more, and to make them part of a plan.

Notes

1. Italian Ministry of Foreign Affairs, *Communità Italiane nel Mondo 1985-1987* (Italian communities around the world 1985–1987), Rome 1988. The data were revised in EURISPES, *Rapporto Italia '96* (Italy report 1996), Rome 1996, pp. 713 ff.

2. See G. Rosoli, "Da Italoamericani ad Euroamericani" (From Italian-Americans to European-Americans), in *XXI Secolo, Studi e Ricerche della Fondazione Giovanni Agnelli* (The twenty-first century: studies and research by the Giovanni Agnelli Foundation), December 1990.

3. M. C. Nascimbene, "Storia della Popolazione Italiana in Argentina (1800–1970): Aspetti Globali" (History of the Italian population in Argentina (1800–1970): general features), in Giovanni Agnelli Foundation, *Euroamericani: La Popolazione di Origine Italiana in Argentina* (European-Americans: the population of Italian origin in Argentina), Turin 1987, p. 511.

4. Cited in AA.VV, "La Business Community Italiana nel Mondo" (The Italian business community worldwide), *Impresa e Stato*, the journal of the Milan

Chamber of Commerce for Industry, Agriculture and Craftsmen (CCIAA), supplement to issue no. 22, June 1993.

5. K. Ciongoli, E. Luttwak, and G. Talese, *"Lobby Tricolore in Cerca d'Autore"* (Italian lobby in search of a client), Roundtable in *liMes, L'America e Noi* (America and Italy), issue no. 4/1996, pp. 241-242.

6. Deputy Minister of Foreign Affairs Piero Fassino, speech given January 13, 1998, at the Forum of the Democratic Left for Italians Abroad.

2

How Italian Is the Universal Church?

Stefano Picciaredda

Pope Wojtyla's accession marked a watershed in the "Italian character" of the Catholic Church. But Italians and the "Roman spirit" are still at the core of Church personnel and government. Italian is the common tongue of the church hierarchy.

Toward the end of his papacy Angelo Roncalli, Pope John XXIII, jotted down a joke that was going around the Vatican: "Angelo (Dell'Acqua) rules; Carlo (Confalonieri) reports; Alfredo (Ottaviani) oversees; Domenico (Tardini) governs; Giovanni (i.e., Pope John XXIII) gives his blessing."[1] The Second Vatican Council was well under way, and Paul VI's thoroughgoing reform of the Roman Curia five years later was still a long way off. In 1962, it seems, the universal Catholic Church was governed by a small group of men on a first-name basis; they were all Italian.

Sixteen years later, in 1978, Karol Wojtyla, the archbishop of Krakow, was raised to the papacy. His election was the culmination of a process of internationalization that was sweeping over the Catholic Church and its government. The choice was a clear break with the past; the last time a non-Italian pope had been elected was in 1522, with Pope Adrian VI of Utrecht. Now that Giovanni is no longer giving his blessing to Domenico, Carlo, and Alfredo, does it still make sense to talk about the Italian character of the Catholic Church? How great a role do Italians, the Italian language, and a special Italian take on things play in the Church at large? And to the extent such an Italian character still survives, in what sense could it be a vehicle for Italian identity throughout the world? The attempt to answer those questions that follows is based on numbers to some degree, but it also draws on interviews, all with Roman sources.

A Marginally Italian Church Government

A quick glance through the *Annuario Pontificio* seems to confirm the impression that Italians are now in the minority.[2] The first indication of this comes from the College of Cardinals. Following the recent appointments made public by John Paul II on January 18, 1998, its ranks include 166 cardinals. But although 40 of them are Italian, only 22 are under 80 years old and therefore eligible to participate in the conclave to elect a new pope (out of a total of 123 eligible cardinals), fewer than from Latin America (24) or other European countries (34). The next conclave will therefore have the smallest number of Italians of any in history.[3] The Italian electors, moreover, do not constitute a monolithic bloc that could be called an "Italian party." In the words of Giancarlo Zizola, it is abundantly clear that "the Italian hegemony over the papacy, already beleaguered by the popes' policy of internationalizing the College of Cardinals after the Second World War, was probably dealt a death blow by the election of the Slavic pope."[4] Cardinal Silvestrini, prefect of the Congregation for the Oriental Churches, acknowledged as much when he wrote,

> [W]ith John Paul II, everything has changed. We have reached beyond the Alps. Anything is possible from here on out, now that we have gotten past that barrier. I think the specific individual will be an increasingly important consideration. Pope Wojtyla was chosen primarily as an individual. Anyone who has seen him at work and heard him speak recognizes in him the fervor and doctrine of a father of the Church, with his unique, charismatic personality. Who knows? We could have a future pope from Latin America, Africa, or somewhere else. Geopolitically, this was a giant qualitative leap forward.[5]

Indeed, the map of the conclave is multicolored with its panoply of nations, even small ones like the Samoan Islands, Vietnam, Benin, Nicaragua and Bosnia-Herzegovina, plainly reflecting Pope Wojtyla's internationalization policy.

Internationalization has made even greater strides within the Roman Curia, the collection of long-standing and recently es-

Figure 2.1

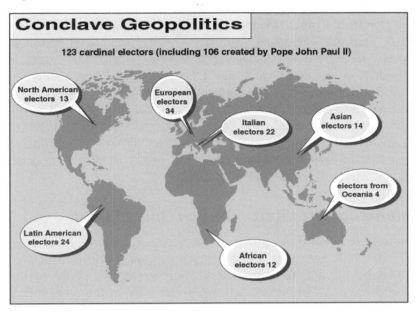

Conclave Geopolitics

123 cardinal electors (including 106 created by Pope John Paul II)

North American electors 13

European electors 34

Italian electors 22

Asian electors 14

electors from Oceania 4

Latin American electors 24

African electors 12

tablished dicasteries (departments) that aid the pontiff in governing the Church. Only three of the nine congregations are headed by Italian cardinals: the Congregation for the Oriental Churches (Achille Silvestrini), the Congregation for the Causes of Saints (Alberto Bovone), and the Congregation for Catholic Education (Pio Laghi). Even the office staff and secretaries are largely non-Italian. Thus, out of 224 Category 1 and Category 2 employees, as the Curia traditionally classifies them, 88, or a little over one-third, are Italians.[6] Dicasteries of fundamental importance, long controlled by Italians, have been placed in the hands of non-Italian prelates, as in the case of the Congregation for the Doctrine of the Faith headed by German Cardinal Ratzinger. Cardinal Gantin of Benin heads the Congregation for Bishops, and Slovak Cardinal Tomko is the prefect of the Congregation for the Evangelization of Peoples, formerly known as the Sacred Congregation de Propaganda Fide.

The only Italian president of the 11 pontifical councils—established after Vatican II at the dicastery level to provide guidance and foster a conciliatory spirit of dialogue and openness toward the contemporary world—is Giovanni Cheli of the Pontifical Council for the Pastoral Care of Migrants and Itinerant Peoples. The Pontifical Council for the Laity is headed by an American, Cardinal Stafford; Nigerian Cardinal Arinze heads the Pontifical Council for Inter-Religious Dialogue; French Cardinal Etchegaray is president of the Pontifical Council for Justice and Peace; and the Pontifical Council for Promoting Christian Unity is headed by Australian Cardinal Cassidy.[7] Italians are even hard to find in the three apostolic tribunals: the Major Penitentiary is Cardinal Baum from Texas; the prefect of the Apostolic Signatura is Gilberto Agustoni of Switzerland; and the dean of the Roman Rota is an Italian, Mario Francesco Pompedda.

Internationalization of Church Government

The rapid opening-up and internationalization of the Church in the late 1960s grew out of the conciliatory spirit and reform promoted by John XXIII. As early as the preparatory phase of the second Vatican Council, which got under way in the second half of 1959, bishops worldwide were asked for their desiderata and, more generally, to express their views "freely and in all sincerity" as to what would be good for the Church. Their answers revealed some dissatisfaction with Rome and the work of the Curia. American and Canadian bishops pointed out Rome's excessive centralization and how little it had been internationalized. Many bishops from various parts of the world shared these concerns; Europeans asked "not to be viewed as mere agents of the Curia."[8]

The prior consultation began a long process of reviewing and rethinking the structure and makeup of Church government, which would continue in the council sessions and culminate, in a sense, in Paul VI's thoroughgoing reform of the Curia in 1967 with the *Regimini Ecclesiae Universae*. As Andrea Riccardi writes, Pope Montini did not want a traditionalist Curia to lead the implementation of Vatican II, which would make the directives meaningless.[9] He wanted a less Roman and more international Curia, which would let itself be led by the pope and enjoyed the respect of Catholic bishops, with new personnel in tune with the times.

Previously, advancement within the Curia came about, with some exceptions, through "lines" or "families" of prelates with a certain shared vision and a tight grip on leadership positions. In this regard the most important change was the reinstatement of the secretariat of state to a position of absolute preeminence. Up until the reform it had been seen as a Vatican office with sweeping powers, but less prestige than the congregations. The *Regimini Ecclesiae Universae* called upon the secretariat to "work directly with the pope in matters relating to the running of the Church as a whole and relations with the dicasteries of the Curia" (Article 19). With its two sections, one for general affairs and the other for relations with governments, the secretariat is the keystone to the entire structure.[10] In practice, its experts draft a report on every issue, separate and apart from the documents prepared by the relevant congregation, which conclude with the recommendations of the secretary of state or his deputy. These recommendations are addressed directly to the pope, who can thus monitor the work of the Curia and make a decision without reference to the information provided by the various dicasteries.[11] The other section—the pope's "State Department"—handles relations with governments and the Vatican's widespread diplomatic activities.

With the reform, diocesan bishops were made part of dicastery plenary assemblies along with the cardinals, to give them a greater say in the final settlement of controversies. Moreover, heads of dicasteries, secretaries and members would serve for five-year terms, enabling the pope to reinstate them, a feature which underscores the control the pope exercises over his Curia. This principle of making positions fixed-term rather than open-ended was put into practice again in 1970, when cardinals over the age of 80 lost the right to vote in conclaves.

The reform had its critics, for failing to do away with so many vestiges of temporalism and introducing a *nouvelle centralisation,* as the French theologian Congar put it.[12] Nevertheless, the reform marked a watershed. As Andrea Riccardi writes:

> The internationalization of the Curia broke up a long-standing sense of unity among the staff that had determined the course of careers, views, and co-optations. Foreigners, often middle-aged, came to Rome with no ties to traditional circles and institutions, and without any existing relationships with each other, intruding on that

sense of group unity. They often stood alone before the pope and their dicastery. Paul VI managed to free Vatican circles from the secret or openly acknowledged communities of interests, but in doing so he dismantled the apparatus that had performed the functions of selection, training and admission. The Roman character, and Italian character, of the Curia had provided a shared language, ecclesiastical culture, and work style. The reformed Curia was to contribute to holding an increasingly complex Catholic world together, as it went through a process of transferring authority to its many parts, or even a breakaway movement. Thus, a less Roman and more international Curia closer to the pope was created, and a new, more collegial work style was introduced.[13]

Islands of Italian Influence

As in the internationalized Curia, Italians are a far from insignificant force in the new multinational, multilingual conclave. To understand the weight and importance of this, perhaps one has to read between the lines. We find that there is almost always an Italian among the trio of prelates who, along with the prefect or president, direct a dicastery. But most of all we find that the secretariat of state, the central importance of which has already been touched on, is very Italian, with Cardinal Angelo Sodano and his deputy, Giovanni-Battista Re (so irreplaceable as to be one of the cardinals *in pectore*, some Vatican-watchers say[14]); Undersecretary Celestino Migliore; Jean-Louis Tauran, the undersecretary for Relations with States, who passes for Italian with his excellent French-accented pronunciation; and the new adviser for General Affairs, Spaniard Pedro Lopez-Quintana. Even the secretariat's staff—from the chief of protocol to attachés to special nuncios—is largely Italian, to a much greater extent than any other dicastery.[15]

Papal diplomacy, the world's oldest, has traditionally been Italian in character. The Holy See currently maintains diplomatic relations with 160 governments, and the nuncio or pronuncio to 104 of them is Italian.[16] But new developments are under way here as well: the number of Italian students attending the Holy

See's college for diplomats, the Pontificia Accademia Ecclesiastica (formerly the school for noble ecclesiastics), is down. Six out of a total of 34 students are Italians, whereas they accounted for at least half in prior years.

What does this presence mean? Clearly, the Italians in the Curia and the conclave do not constitute a party, a monolithic bloc, or even a lobby intent on sponsoring candidatures and shared policy goals. The days of the "Roman Party" are long gone, when it could place restrictions on the pope's teachings and advocate its own conservative policy. Nevertheless, Italians are strategically placed: a minority, but a very widespread one. They are still the best-represented nationality in the conclave and the Curia, and among bishops (585 out of 4,319)[17] and missionaries. They are a core presence in the Vatican and constitute a connective tissue. In a sense, they perform the same role as the Italian language: not an official, but an unofficial, role.

The rules of procedure of the Roman Curia have been in force since 1992 and are the culmination of the reform begun four years earlier by John Paul II with his *Pastor Bonus* encyclical. Title 12, Article 128 states that "the dicasteries shall draft documents in the Italian language, but the languages most widely spoken today can also be used." Latin is still the official language of the Holy See, but many dicasteries, especially the more recently established ones, admit to never having written a line of Latin and signing off on documents in Italian, letting them be translated elsewhere at a later time. Thus, even though Spanish and English are the first languages of many dicastery officials, Italian is spoken at the staff meetings. Based on a rough estimate, at least half the cardinals in the next conclave will speak Italian fluently, and many more will have a passive knowledge. Italian is the common language, then, albeit unofficially. The main edition of the Holy See's official publication is in Italian; weekly editions of the Osservatore Romano also appear in French, English, Portuguese, Spanish, German, and Polish.

Another important point to consider is the number of Italian priests and personnel working throughout the world. There are 16,314 Italian missionaries (men and women) spread over five continents, with only 10 percent working in European countries or North America. The rest are concentrated in developing countries and the Third World: 45 percent live in Latin America,

Central America, and the Caribbean; 31 percent in Africa; and 12 percent in Asia and Oceania. They are religious (7,432 women and 6,418 men), *fidei donum* priests (1,052), and lay assistants (1,008), as well as contemplatives, consecrated persons, and members of congregations not included in the count. In addition, 91 Italian bishops preside over foreign dioceses.[18] (Only Spanish missionaries outnumber Italians, with about 20,000.) They are spread throughout a wide variety of areas, both where the Church has a long-standing presence and in recently evangelized areas. Italian missionaries are easy to find in the Southern Hemisphere, where their special character makes them stand out. Missionaries are often the population's last line of defense when governments break down and violence becomes widespread, as occurred recently in Sierra Leone, Burundi, and the Congo (the former Zaire).

Lay religious movements born out of local needs take on a broader vocation from Rome and Italy and spread to many countries. The Focolare Movement, founded by Chiara Lubich, and the Community of Saint Egidio scarcely need to be mentioned.[19] Such movements are also ambassadors of the "Italian spirit" in their own way.

Romans by Adoption

> Italy! Rome! These names have always been near and dear to me. The history of Poland and Church history are full of events that draw Rome and Italy near and make them dear to me; I might even say make them my own. Krakow, the city I come from, is known as "the Polish Rome." As I come from "the Polish Rome" to Rome the Eternal City, I hope that as bishop of Rome I will be able to serve . . . everyone.

These words spoken by John Paul II to the faithful assembled in Saint Peter's Square a few days after his election, as cited by Marco Impagliazzo in a revealing study on Pope Wojtyla and Italy,[20] are no accident. They could almost be an appeal for acceptance by the Roman faithful, who were accustomed to having an Italian bishop. In fact, they are the words of a bishop from the East putting down deep roots in a land that does not feel foreign or strange to him.

　　Karol Wojtyla was no newcomer to Rome at the time he was elected. He had studied at the Angelicum, the Dominican university, and had been an active council father. His thinking and commitment to Italy would deepen over the years. A fairly specific geopolitical vision of Italy in the Mediterranean and European context would arise out of the way he handled being bishop of Rome and head of the Church as a whole. But he felt like a Roman before then. He shares that feeling with hundreds of bishops and cardinals from all over the world. A survey of Rome's pontifical universities reveals that a third of the approximately 3,000 non-Italian bishops studied in Rome.[21] The Jesuits' Gregorian University alone boasts 768 bishops and 59 cardinals among its alumni. Of the bishops, 310 are American, 39 are African, 52 are Asian, 10 are from Oceania, and 357 are European (no information is available on how many of them are Italian). The geographical distribution of the cardinals is similar. The Pontifical Lateran University has trained 268 bishops (perhaps half are non-Italian), and the University Urbaniana de Propaganda Fide about 100. Another 72 attended other universities: the Dominicans' Pontifical University of St. Thomas Aquinas (the Angelicum), the Pontifical Salesian University, and the Pontificium Athenaeum Antonianum of the Franciscans.

　　Studying in Rome leaves its mark, apart from the quality of the training. These thousand bishops learned Italian, soaked up the spirit of the city, were introduced to Italian things, rediscovered Christianity's landmarks and origins, and gained firsthand knowledge of the workings of the Church's central government, the Curia. They discussed it, criticized it, and presaged change. More than that, during their studies foreign seminarians and religious undertake work as part of the local Church in parishes, assistance centers, and Roman communities, in downtown Rome and outlying areas. Studying in Rome also enables them to see their own country in a special light, from the vantage point of Rome. Priests and religious who spend time in Rome, then, soak up a "Roman spirit" and take it away with them.

　　Rome is also home to the motherhouses of most religious institutions, even those whose top officials are not Italian. Foreigners are more prevalent in such institutions as well: only 22 of the 67 orders and societies for men with more than 500 members have one or two Italians among their leaders. As a result, Rome draws foreign religious visiting their superiors, and bishops making *ad limina* visits and convened for the various continental synods; following on the African (1995) and American (1997) synods, the Synod of Asian Bishops was held this past April. Most of the more than 14,000 students enrolled at pontifical universities are foreign. All cardinals are Romans by adoption; according to an ancient custom, each cardinal is a priest of Rome and member of the order of bishops, parish priests, or deacons, depending on the suburbicarian diocese or church assigned to him.

But spending years in the shadow of the dome of Saint Peter's is not the only way to be adopted by Rome. One notable example is Joseph Ratzinger, the prefect of the Congregation for the Doctrine of the Faith. His youth was spent in Bavaria, not Rome, which he did not see until 1962 at age 35. He had this to say about that first visit, many years ago now: "I did not feel like a foreigner here at all, since from the beginning this city with its past and present had been an essential part of the world in which I grew up, was educated, and began my vocational journey."[22] For Cardinal Ratzinger, Rome is an essential part of his world, even when it is far away. This bears witness to a special quality possessed by the Italian capital, which those who make their home there have difficulty getting a handle on, in part because it does not quite coincide with the overworked rhetoric of the "Eternal City." A man with a profound knowledge of Rome, the French historian Philippe Boutry, wrote of his experience as a foreigner in the city, that

> the first and fundamental discovery a foreigner in Rome makes seems to be the city's universality: the universality of the Church and the papacy, the clergy, religious and seminarians from all nations; the universality of customs and the languages heard; the universality of the liturgy, art and Catholic symbolism; and the sense that the city's churches and monuments, Christian and otherwise, belong to the universal history of mankind.

When you come into contact with Rome, you have the sensation or certainty that you are not a foreigner there. Boutry goes on to say, "Rome is perhaps the only city in the world that gives the visitor that sense of spontaneous familiarity or déjà vu, that is, a sense of existential community and cultural, if not religious, communion. Perhaps that is why travelling to Rome is so often an unforgettable experience. It brings out profound individual, cultural or spiritual traits in a previously unknown city. . . ."[23]

The experience of these exceptional foreigners clearly shows how much Rome is part of one who is Catholic and is steeped in Western culture. Rome's universal character is what makes that possible. Perhaps that universal character, which is why so many foreigners discover their roots there in a kind of "adoption by Rome," is becoming more pronounced as the Church becomes more international, that is, more Roman and less Italian. Rome is not Geneva or the United Nations building in New York, and the Vatican does not fit the model of large international organizations like the United Nations, the UN Food and Agriculture Organization (FAO), or federations of nations, which is what the Church's Ecumenical Council is, in a certain sense. Rome's special character is its universality, and that makes it an important vehicle for the export of Italian identity throughout the world.

Notes

1. John XXIII, *Lettere 1958-1963* (Letters 1958-1963), Rome 1978, p. 518.

2. *Annuario Pontificio 1997*, Vatican City. This "yearbook" is the source for all data on the College of Cardinals, the Roman Curia, papal representatives, and institutes of consecrated life. It is published by a special office of the Vatican's Secretariat of State.

3. Karol Wojtyla was voted in by 111 electors, 28 or about one-fourth of whom were Italian. Today that ratio has gone down to one-sixth, but in the early 1900s 61 percent of the cardinals were Italian. They lost the absolute majority under Pius XII, and the one-third required to control any election under Paul VI. See G. Zizola, *Il Successore* (The successor), Roma-Bari 1997, Laterza.

4. Ibid., p. 108.

5. "Quando il Vaticano Pensa il Mondo" (When the Vatican thinks of the world), Round Table in *liMes, Le Città di Dio*, issue no. 3/1993, p. 27.

6. In many dicasteries the "staff" is made up of the Category 1 personnel, who hold the positions of office manager, research assistant, and secretary, together with the president of the council or prefect of the congregation, who

meet periodically to conduct office business. The most "Italian" of the congregations, with 10 Italian employees out of a total of 16, is the Congregation for Divine Worship and the Discipline of the Sacraments, which is headed by new Chilean Cardinal Medina and is responsible for "the regulation and fostering of the sacred liturgy, and the discipline and celebration the sacraments." The least Italian, on the other hand, is the Congregation for Bishops, headed by African Cardinal Gantin, with 4 Italian employees out of a total of 18.

7. Cardinal Cassidy's is the most international of the councils, with only one Italian on staff. By contrast, Cor Unum, the pontifical council headed by German Archbishop Cordes that coordinates aid initiatives and acts as a go-between with Catholic institutions and international humanitarian organizations, has 5 Italians out of a staff of 8. For a systematic treatment of the operation and rules governing the Curia, see C. Cardia, *Il Governo dell Chiesa* (Church government), Bologna 1993, Il Mulino; and N. del Re, *La Curia Romana, Lineamenti Storico-Giuridici* (The Roman Curia: Historical and legal overview), Rome 1970.

8. See A. Riccardi, *Il Potere del Papa, da Pio XII a Giovanni Paolo II* (The Power of the pope from Pius XII to John Paul II), Roma-Bari 1993, Laterza, p. 205.

9. Ibid., p. 293.

10. See A. Acerbi, *Paolo VI, Il Papa che Baciò la Terra* (Paul VI: The pope who kissed the ground), Cinisello Balsamo 1997, Ed. S. Paolo, p. 84.

11. Ibid.

12. See Y. M. Congar, *Remarques Générales* (General observations), in *Paul VI et la Modernité dans l'Eglise* (Paul VI and modernity in the Church), Rome 1984, p. 852.

13. In A. Riccardi, *Il Potere del Papa*, p. 293.

14. See L. Accattoli, "Quelle Nomine 'In Pectore' " (The "In Pectore" appointments)," *Corriere della Sera*, January 19, 1998.

15. Italians account for 30 out of a total of 47 staff.

16. Other diplomatic representations include the 15 apostolic delegations (8 Italians), the 24 representative offices maintained by the Vatican at governmental and nongovernmental organizations, the European Community, and the Organization for Security and Cooperation in Europe (OSCE).

17. Source: Central Bureau of Statistics of the Secretariat of State.

18. Source: FIDES, the international agency of the Congregation for the Evangelization of Peoples.

19. The Focolare Movement, founded by Chiara Lubich in the early 1940s, promotes interreligious dialogue and universal unity; its information service is

headquartered in Rome. The Community of St. Egidio, founded in Rome in 1968 and headquartered there, is devoted to serving the poor and working toward peace; it has mediated many agreements between warring factions.

20. M. Impaghiazzo, "Perché il Papa Polacco Vuole Salvare l'Unità d'Italia" (Why the Polish pope wants to save Italian unity), *liMes, A Che Serve l'Italia,* issue no. 4/1994, p. 91.

21. Some figures are necessarily approximations, as the principal pontifical universities do not have accurate records of their former students and their current positions. In some cases the secretary generals were able to provide only estimates.

22. Cited by A. Riccardi, keynote address of "Alla Scuola della Verità: I Settanta Anni di Joseph Ratzinger"(At the school of truth: Joseph Ratzinger's seventy years), Edizioni San Paolo, 1997, held in Rome at the Basilica of Santa Maria in Trastevere, December 1997.

23. Ibid.

3

Pacific Calling Mediterranean: A Future for Our Ports

Adalberto Vallega

Italy's ability to recapture its former status in the Mediterranean will depend chiefly on Genoa, Trieste, and Gioia Tauro. Container traffic is the price of admission to the major intercontinental shipping networks.

The geopolitical face and geostrategic landscape of the Mediterranean are changing fast. For various reasons—ranging from its renewed geographic importance to the links being forged with the Balkans and the Black Sea—Italy is taking on a more important role in the Mediterranean, which is likewise experiencing a resurgence of international interest. As in other parts of the world, change is the result of strategies adopted by regional organizations (the European Union in Italy's case) and economic processes.

Maritime ports are taking on a vastly different role from the one they played up to the early 1980s, not because they (at least the biggest ones) did not perform functions of value in international relations, but because the nature and scope of the functions they do perform have begun to change and are starting to take on special geopolitical significance. Against this background, Italy is rousing interest because several of its ports are exhibiting such strong growth that they appear at the least to be pointing the way toward new status for Italy internationally and a pivotal role for Italy in the Mediterranean. The source of this impression is the media, which has portrayed a number of ports—especially Genoa, Voltri, and Gioia Tauro—as revolutionary ports of entry, and the international trade press, which is increasingly highlighting the leading role Italy plays in maritime routes to, or transiting through, the Mediterranean Sea.

What is the nature of this change, and what geopolitical significance could it have? The answers are not to be found in the numbers. Genoa, Italy's largest port, ranks among medium to small ports with total traffic of 40–45 million tons annually, a far cry from gargantuan Rotterdam (300 million tons annually) and even from the medium-sized ports of Antwerp and Marseilles with annual traffic of around 100 million tons.

The figures for containers—a key factor for today's ports—do not alter the picture substantially.[1] The praise lavished on Genoa by the media for topping one million containers in 1997 to take the lead among Mediterranean ports is well earned, but Genoa is still a small port when compared with ports worldwide. Genoa handles roughly one-fifteenth the volume that Hong Kong does (more than 13 million containers) and trails far behind medium-to-large ports (5 million-10 million containers). At best, it can aspire to the ranks of medium-sized ports (2 million-5 million containers). When it succeeds, it will still rank about twentieth in the world.

The traffic structure at Italian ports, moreover, is not characteristic of a country with established international maritime transport markets. Unloading constitutes four-fifths of traffic totaling around 350-400 million tons per year, made up of petroleum and natural gas, coal, and grain headed for the domestic economy. This is a sign of dependence on foreign exports, not market success. Commercial traffic—a key component of port traffic consisting of intermediate goods and finished products—does not exceed one-fourth of total traffic. This ratio is low in relation to some Northern European port fronts, like the Netherlands.

Italian Ports as International Nodes

The function Italian ports can potentially perform in the changing Mediterranean cannot be sketched out based on these factors, then, but on how their functions will change and what the prospects are for plugging into high-value-added traffic networks, namely containerized traffic. The question is whether Italian ports will be able to take on a transshipment and redistribution role serving the Mediterranean and Europe for traffic arriving from the great Pacific markets. In the postmodern economy, what matters is a port's ability to plug into international shipping networks in a redistribution capacity. This redistribution function makes ports nodes, or branch points. With the globalization of international mercantile transport, that is why they exist.

The stage is set for a change. Traffic generated by the Western Pacific and then transported eastbound to North America or west-

Figure 3.1

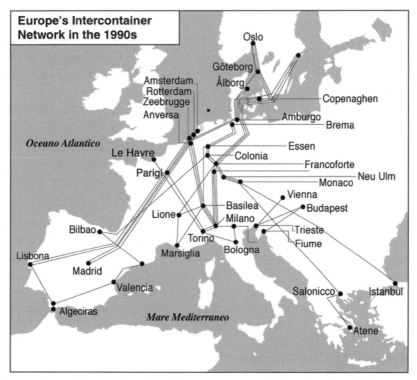

Europe's Intercontainer Network in the 1990s

bound to Europe is climbing very steadily. The four dragons (South Korea, Taiwan, Singapore, and Hong Kong), nestled between a proven giant (Japan) and an awakening one (China), are turning that area into the maritime center of the world, wresting that banner away from the North Atlantic, which had held it firmly in its grasp for two centuries. The long-term projected growth of international transport using large oceangoing vessels is based primarily on what is happening with the routes leading from the Suez Canal to Southeast Asia and the Far East.

The Mediterranean is answering these urgent calls from the Pacific. The proof is in the rise in intra-Mediterranean redistribution traffic for goods arriving over ocean routes. The expansion of companies like Med Feeder, Intermodal Cyprus, Sarlis Container Services, and Sea Malta is a sign of substantial revitalization. Traffic redistribution circuits are also developing well-defined geographical features. One circuit links the ports on the northern coast of the

Tyrrhenian Sea with Marseilles and Barcelona; a second links ports in the northwestern Mediterranean with the Maghreb region; a number of routes fan out from Trieste; a circuit links Eastern Mediterranean ports (Piraeus, Istanbul, Izmir, and Alexandria) with Italian ports like La Spezia and Salerno, and vice versa. A fairly intricate geography is taking shape that vaguely resembles the geographies that grew up in Southeast Asia.

Where can the Italian port framework start to begin taking on a leading role? This question must be looked at in terms of two components: industrial traffic and commercial traffic.

Industrial Functions: The Passing of an Era

Starting in the mid-1950s and for 20 years thereafter, Italy was a central figure in industrial traffic, consisting chiefly of minerals and sources of energy. The reason was the spread of port industrial areas in the Mediterranean, especially the northwestern part. Italy rode this wave of expansion, building iron and steel works, refineries, petrochemical plants, and ever-larger steam power plants near its ports. From Genoa Cornigliano to Naples, from Priola Melilli to Ravenna, Mestre, and Trieste—just to name the best known—an array of supporting industrial areas grew up around the ports. This process reached its peak in the second half of the 1960s, when analysts scarcely even considered commercial traffic relevant, their vision clouded as it was by the big numbers generated by raw materials traffic. The industrial area with its specialized port terminals was among the most eloquent testimony to vigorous economic growth. France did even better than Italy during that period, setting up the Fos industrial area as an important component of the Marseilles port system. It covered more than 7,000 hectares with room for expansion up to 20,000. Spanish ports like Barcelona, Tarragona, and Seville were no less successful.

That era seems very long ago now. Few of those industrial areas have survived; some were dismantled and laboriously reconverted, while others struggle on, biding time until the inevitable occurs, like Genoa Cornigliano. Domestic demand for the two basic production sectors for intermediate goods—iron and oil—topped off in the late 1970s. Developing countries, including those on the southern Mediterranean seaboard, also started building various types of industrial areas with equipment for assembling and manufacturing finished products. The establishment of free trade areas stimulated this process. Only one conclusion can be drawn: there is no future in industrial traffic and port industrialization. In the environment of the global marketplace these factors will not play a significant role in northern Mediterranean port scenarios, at least as far as Italy is concerned.

Containers: The Mediterranean Takes Off

Thus, attention shifted to containers, the principal instrument of commercial transport and international maritime relations. When the Mediterranean's first *scatolone,* or "big box," came ashore at Genoa in 1969, it was met with skepticism. Economists and engineers agreed that it had no future and continued to sing the praises of the port's industrial functions. And yet the "Battle of the Atlantic" had been fought three years earlier, when cutthroat competition had broken out among the then-biggest companies over container traffic between the United States and Europe. The success of Rotterdam, Antwerp, Felixtowe, Le Havre, and other European ports operating on the containerized traffic market dates from that time.

It was not until 1975, with the reopening of the Suez Canal, that better prospects opened up for the Mediterranean other than to be an area bypassed by the great containerized traffic routes. When the first containerships came through the reopened canal, the Mediterranean was essentially virgin territory, even though the same kind of ships had sailed it before, entering through Gibraltar. Maritime companies therefore set about formulating strategies without great enthusiasm, and ports began outfitting terminals and developing new organizational models, encountering obstacles along the way that were very difficult to overcome because they reflected a political showdown that was particularly intense in France and Italy. The reason: containers forced ports to adopt organizational models that called for private management. The spread of containerized traffic in the Mediterranean was therefore linked to an internal conflict, in which the stakes—in the bipolar climate of the Cold War—were political control over major ports.

As in every other area, containerized port geography in the

Table 3.1
World's Largest Containerized Ports (1996)
(in thousands of TEUs)

Ports	Thousands of TEUs[a]
1. Hong Kong	13,460
2. Singapore	12,950
3. Kaohsiung	5,063
4. Rotterdam	5,007
5. Busan	4,684
6. Long Beach	3,067
7. Hamburg	3,053
8. Los Angeles	2,683
9. Antwerp	2,620
10. Yokohama	2,400
11. Tokyo	2,290
12. Keelung	2,275
13. Dubai	2,274
14. New York	2,270
15. Felixtowe	2,060
16. Kobe	2,056
17. Shanghai	1,930
18. Manila	1,918
19. San Juan (Puerto Rico)	1,600
20. Bremen	1,550
21. Oakland	1,498
22. Seattle	1,473
23. Algeciras	1,306
24. Norfolk	1,141
25. Charleston	1,079
26. Tacoma	1,073
27. Le Havre	1,020
28. La Spezia	970
29. Genoa	826
30. Barcelona	770

Source: Le Marin
[a] One TEU is equivalent to one 20-foot-long container 10 feet wide and 10 feet high.

Mediterranean took shape through a combination of three functions. The first function was that of *local market*, characterized by traffic fanning inland from the port. Thus, the ports on the northern coast of the Tyrrhenian Sea, together with Venice and Ravenna, served the Po River Valley market. Southern Italy was likewise served by Naples, Salerno, and Bari, while Marseilles had a first-rate market in the Rhone corridor, and Barcelona, the only truly world-class metropolis on the Mediterranean, became the hub of the prime Catalan market. But, understandably, this local function was limited by the size of the regional market served by the individual ports. Italian ports, moreover, especially those on the northern coast of the Tyrrhenian Sea, were seriously compromised by the lines of penetration from the ports on Europe's Northern Range, i.e., the impressive array of ports extending from Hamburg to Le Havre. So-called block trains (trains hauling only containers) shuttled to and from Milan, Rotterdam, and Antwerp, thus eroding the Italian ports' "natural" market.

This last factor brings us to the second function performed by containerized ports: *international transit*. It was clear right from the 1960s that penetration into Europe by northern Mediterranean ports would be much more difficult with containers than it had been with conventional commercial traffic. First, there was the geographic obstacle of having to cross the Alps with fast freight trains. But that was not the main cause, on closer examination, because the Northern Range ports successfully penetrated into Italy in spite of the mountain crossings. Two other factors were much more important: (1) the supply of port facilities and services was decidedly better on the Northern Range than on the Southern European port front, and (2) the rail system was much more efficiently organized in Northern Europe than in Italy, especially as far as freight traffic was concerned. In addition, the northern member countries of the European Community, and later the European Union, have always managed to limit international rail line improvement programs that worked to the advantage of the countries south of the mountains.

The third function performed by ports is the so-called *feeder function*, or the redistribution by sea of goods delivered to a given port over land or sea routes. In practice, ports performing a feeder function act as the point where long ocean routes connect with shorter routes. The large ship calls at the port and unloads containers, which are reloaded onto small sea carriers called "feeder ships" and transported to nearby ports. In the meantime, traffic delivered to the port of call is loaded onto the oceangoing ship. It was clear as early as the late 1960s that, given the limits of the local market and the obstacles to penetrating the European transit mar-

Figure 3.2

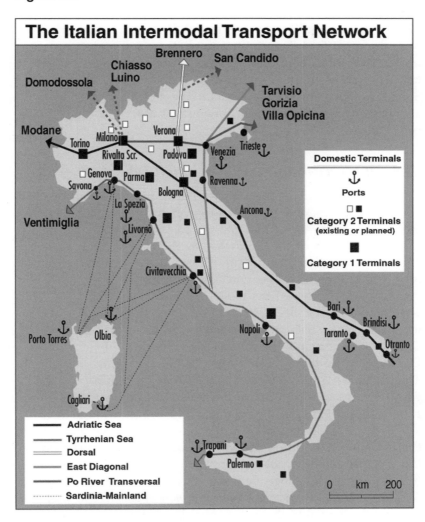

ket, Northern Mediterranean ports would have to view the feeder market as essential to their development.

Only two ports stood out in this regard. Near Gibraltar, Algeciras became the Mediterranean's most important transshipment node, because world market leader Sea-Land selected it as its Mediterranean base for ships in transit from the Pacific and Indian Oceans to the Atlantic, and vice versa. The second port was

Fos. In the late 1960s, as soon as it became clear that the era of big industrial areas was over, the French government decided to modify certain receiving structures at Fos, which had originally been designed for industrial transport, to accommodate container traffic. Thus, big shipping companies called at this new port, creating heavy transshipment traffic. Italian ports like Leghorn and La Spezia, key players in the containerization of the 1970s and 1980s, also began performing feeder functions, but they could not compete with Algeciras and Fos.

The Mediterranean's Place in Global Strategies

This general picture of the Mediterranean basin during the 1970s and 1980s, the period it was taking off in the container market, took shape at the same time that the basin was becoming the central battleground of the Cold War, with the associated phenomenon of international terrorism. The Mediterranean was divided into two groups of routes entering through the Suez. The westbound route represented the Western alliance, while the other routes were bound for the Black Sea and from there along the Danube Valley on Soviet river-barges. The Soviet Union sought ways to consolidate its position in the containerized market along the imperial Danube-Suez-Indian Ocean route. In the meantime it built the Trans-Siberian Railway to move containers from Europe to the Pacific, with the idea of luring traffic away from the western companies operating between the Atlantic and Far East through Suez.

To understand how that context has changed, one must look at the pressures exerted on the Mediterranean by globalization and the collapse of the bipolar geopolitical model. The latter has affected ports in three incisive ways.

First, ships have become bigger and more efficient. The year 1997 marked the arrival of the era of specialized ships capable of carrying more than 6,000 containers. These enormous platforms—more than 300 yards long with at least 15 decks and tiny crews—can sail at 22-23 knots or faster. These mighty ships need to call at as few ports as possible, thus giving strong impetus to redistribution transport and feeders. Feeder ships, for their part, are also evolving to become faster and carry larger loads.

Second, individual containers and their contents can be tracked in real time using modern information systems. Two groups of transport operators have taken advantage of this technology. The first is made up of maritime shipping companies or other kinds of operators (e.g., large rail companies) that act as "global transportation operators" (i.e., handling overland transport from the port to the final destination, or from the point the traffic originates to the port, thus providing "door to door" service). The second group, "global logistics operators," are of more recent vintage and have taken on such an important role as to ensure they will be key players in coming decades. In addition to handling shipment from point of origin to final destination, they also carry out operations traditionally performed by manufacturers: product completion (assembly, painting, labeling, etc.), packing, product placement in commercial distribution channels, quality control, and so on. This strategy has been successfully implemented by major companies, the "global superstars" like Maersk, P & O Nedlloyd, Evergreen, Hanjin/Senator, and the legendary Sea-Land. Companies that are even more colossal are being established as a result of a tidal wave of mergers in 1997. Worldwide containerized traffic, which now constitutes the entirety of commercial maritime transport, will thus be controlled by an ever smaller number of players.

Third, with the progress in information systems and standardized transport technologies, *internal nodes have become widespread and well established throughout the western world under different names from country to country* ("load centers" in the United States, "plates-formes de frêt" in France, "interporti" in Italy). In practice, they are structures equipped to transship containers among the various modes of surface transportation (trains, trucks, or river-barges), handle the contents of an individual container, and perform any other function requested by the global logistics operator. The port competes with these internal nodes for transshipment functions, loading and unloading operations, and distribution. The international operator can choose to have these operations carried out at the port or at an inland node, transferring the load there. The port, therefore, is just another node within a system of nodes. On one hand, it must compete with the internal nodes, and on the other it must be integrated into the network of nodes if it wants to be in a position to seize opportunities as they arise.

With the globalization of transportation and the mergers that accompanied it, the Mediterranean market has taken on a skeletal

Table 3.2
World's Largest and Europe's Largest Ports (1994)
(in millions of tons of traffic)

Worldwide port rankings	Millions of tons of traffic
Rotterdam	294
Singapore	290
Chiba	174
Kobe	171
Shanghai	166
Hong Kong	147
Houston	141
Nagoya	137
Yokohama	128
Antwerp	108
Other European ports	
Marseilles	91
Hamburg	68
Le Havre	54
London	51
Amsterdam	48
Tees and Hartlepool	43
Grimsby/Immingham	41
Genoa	39
Trieste	38
Algeciras	32

Source: Italian National Bureau of Statistics (ISTAT)

structure of a system of nodes. As Balkan and Central European markets are deregulated and grow, they are discovering a natural gateway in the Adriatic ports of call. The Black Sea, a vast and important economic zone, is becoming more and more integrated with the Mediterranean. Eastern Mediterranean markets are being developed. The European Union is implementing, albeit with great difficulty, the policy decisions made in 1996 at the Third Euro-Mediterranean Conference, designed to bring about the creation of the Mediterranean Free Trade Area. Although the United Nations' 1975 Mediterranean Plan of Action has resulted in almost completely ineffectual treaties and protocols, it has helped strengthen relations in the region. In short, within the Mediterranean basin and elsewhere, change is taking place and strategies are being developed that will have a profound impact on ports.

Transshipment

The signs are there, especially in the transshipment sector. Port supply for containerized transport in the Mediterranean is up substantially in the 1990s. Genoa's satellite port of Voltri is operational. Gioia Tauro, which was originally conceived as an iron and steel port, has debuted on the container market, specializing in transshipment. Spanish ports have expanded, and there are signs of progress in the Central and Eastern Mediterranean. The more port supply increases, the more important it is to provide the port with a good feeder transport structure, to make it an efficient connection point between ocean routes and medium- and short-haul shipping. At the same time, the expansion of maritime redistribution transport, as touched on above, provides plenty of room for these kinds of strategies.

Although other ports also perform transshipment functions to some degree, the trade press has focused on four key players at this new functional stage for Mediterranean ports: two new ports, Genoa Voltri and Gioia Tauro, and two established ports, Algeciras and Malta. Malta's leading role is the spearhead of expanding traffic in the Eastern Mediterranean and the Black Sea, eloquent testimony to the new economic and political weight of the eastbound route.

Transit

The system of ports as nodes oriented toward the sea, performing the function of redistributing ocean traffic onto short routes, is a complicated one, but it generates relatively believable scenarios. Difficult questions and uncertain answers arise, however, when the system of ports as nodes is looked at from another angle, namely as performing the function of a point of transit to inland nodes, and thus in terms of the role ports play within the systems of inland nodes that form Europe's skeletal structure. The block trains leaving the new port of Genoa Voltri for the heart of Europe in 1997 were seen as a sign of route reversal: the Italian port system was seemingly no longer the victim of penetration by Northern

Range ports and was capable of standing up to competitors like Le Havre, Antwerp, and Rotterdam, which had been considered unbeatable until then.

One point has to be made before going on to address this issue. Transit does not hinge upon either transport by river or transport over the road. Growth may occur in container transit over waterways—the Rhone and Rhine going north and south, and the Danube and Rhine going east and west—but it will remain confined to small amounts of freight with limited added value. The road network that supports international transit bound for Italy has matured, and over-the-road trucking cannot handle container traffic of the order of magnitude we are beginning to see. Over-the-road trucking, therefore, cannot play much more of a role than it currently does.

The outlook is very bright, on the other hand, for rail transport. Great strides have been made in the technologies for moving containers from ship to train and from train to truck. The era of fast freight trains has gotten off to a successful start, and the so-called global superstars are investing in rail transport. Big overland transport companies are responding by restructuring and intensifying capital investment in an attempt to compete with maritime companies as global logistics operators. It is a complicated game with an uncertain outcome, but it is a sign of how economic and political weight has shifted in relations among the different parts of Europe.

In discussing the relationships among the various European port fronts in relation to rail transport, one therefore has to look at the network of lines offered by the major international operators. In the mid-1990s the network run by Intercontainer, Europe's largest company, gave it a presence of great geopolitical significance. The network was made up of lines running south from Sweden with a central corridor bound for Milan. This node, together with Turin and Lyons, constituted a kind of southern advance base. Only lines of relatively limited importance ran south from there, whether to the southwest (to the Iberian Peninsula) or, especially, to the southeast (the Balkan Peninsula). Even so, very significantly from the geopolitical standpoint, there was no line running down the Italian peninsula.

Italy's prospects for increasing its influence along routes penetrating into the heart of Europe thus have this shaky and uncertain foundation to build on. Clearly, the outlook is bright for Trieste, which can work toward the goals of recovering its role as Central Europe's port on the Mediterranean and becoming a port for the Balkans, if that region moves toward stable economic restructuring. But while the outlook is bright in and of itself, it is dimmed by the network available to handle fast, specialized traffic like containers. The route bound for Vienna and Budapest is definitely sound, as the Intercontainer lines indicate. The route running through the Balkans bound for Greece and Turkey, however, is practically nonexistent and will require substantial international cooperation and considerable investment to reach its full potential. Essentially, scenarios dealing with this route can only be long-term and are characterized by valid unknowns with pervasive ramifications.

The east-central route over the Brenner Pass, as well as the central (St. Gotthard) and west-central (Sempione) routes, are well connected with the Po River Valley nodes transversely (Turin-Venice-Trieste) and dorsally (Verona-Padua-Bologna), and together they form the most strategically important skeletal structure for Italy's future prospects. Once over the Alps, they connect with the great Rhine corridor, the lines bound for Northern Europe and the branches running to Central Europe. They would, however, have to be thoroughly renovated for high-speed freight trains, much more than the European Union member countries have agreed to. Last, the Fréjus line, which has become crucial to high-speed passenger connections between Italy and France, will also play a prime strategic role in the transport of containers, as it feeds into the Paris-London route.

Networks of Nodes and the Geopolitical Fabric

Italy's success in carving out a place for itself in the areas of high-value-added traffic that will take shape within the Mediterranean basin and in relations between the Mediterranean and other areas—first and foremost the Western Pacific—will clearly depend on more than ports. Lines of transportation and internal nodes will also be important. The entire system must develop in concert, while giving each individual node ample freedom to act so that it can develop to its full potential. In the 1980s Italy came up with the National Transportation Plan, which was built

Figure 3.3

Maritime Petroleum Transport Routes in the Mid-1990s

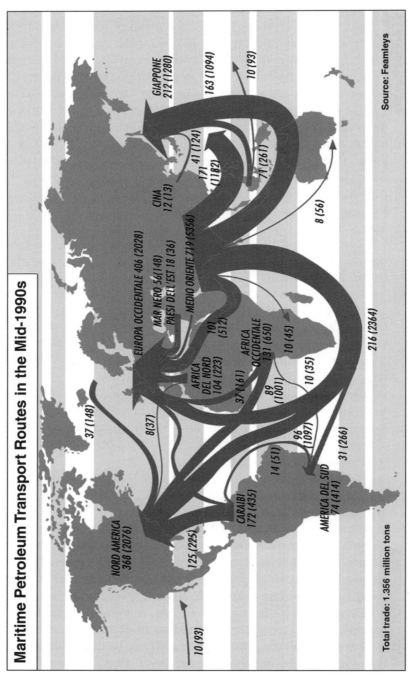

GIAPPONE 212 (1280)

163 (1094)

10 (93)

41 (124)

171 (1182)

71 (261)

CINA 12 (13)

8 (56)

EUROPA OCCIDENTALE 406 (2028)

MAR NERO 56 (148)

PAESI DEL'EST 18 (36)

MEDIO ORIENTE 719 (5356)

101 (512)

AFRICA OCCIDENTALE 131 (650)

10 (45)

AFRICA DEL NORD 104 (223)

37 (61)

89 (1001)

10 (35)

216 (2364)

37 (148)

8 (37)

96 (1097)

14 (51)

31 (266)

CARAIBI 172 (435)

AMERICA DEL SUD 74 (414)

NORD AMERICA 368 (2076)

125 (225)

10 (93)

Source: Fearnleys

Total trade: 1.356 million tons

around the concepts of a "multimodal corridor" and "load centers." The plan has been ineffectual and was in fact misguided from the start by requiring that the system be set up and run exclusively by a state-owned operator.

The frame of reference, therefore, has changed radically due to technological factors, as touched on above, and the advent of international economic operators that go well beyond the purview of governments. A thorough updating of Italian policy is therefore inevitable to

- unleash entrepreneurship in the port and overland transport sectors (especially rail transport) and in internal nodes for container transport; and

- create a favorable environment for investment from within Italy and abroad.

This aspect of the problem has consequences for the geopolitics of mainstream international relations. The repercussions for Italy in the Mediterranean and elsewhere will vary, depending on which routes are favored and which nodes (ports or internal nodes) get developed. The traffic will be generated by the Western Pacific (i.e., Southeast Asia and the Far East), as that will be the maritime center of the world. Right behind it will come the developing markets of the former Communist countries (i.e., the Balkans, Central Europe, and the former Soviet republics). Essentially, everything points toward the East, operating first and foremost through the Suez Canal—for connections served by the major ocean routes, which are the stronghold of the global superstars and the proving ground of the new-generation ships—and, second, over the Black Sea route toward the developing markets.

Italy's response to these urgent calls can focus on three port complexes: the North Adriatic, for connections to Central Europe and the Balkan Peninsula; the ports on the northern coast of the Tyrrhenian Sea, once equipped for overland transport in the northwestern Mediterranean, to penetrate the rich European transit market; and the ports of southern Italy, a prime example of which is Gioia Tauro, to establish itself in the transshipment market. Successful ports will probably see the creation of logistical platforms clustering together end-of-cycle industrial operations (such as product completion and preparation for shipment) and high-value-added services, such as banking, insurance, and quality control, all made possible by the convergence of traffic flows, transshipment, and container handling. These technologically advanced logistical platforms, plugged into the global networks that govern international commerce, will make the port a typical example of the traffic node in postmodern society. They will also certainly be laden with geopolitical significance, marking the country's status on the international stage. But only a few ports and internal nodes will be selected to perform such high-level functions. It is a fascinating exercise to predict whether such structures can evolve within Italy and how best to favor their development, but there are so many possible outcomes that such an exercise runs the risk of straying into mere speculation.

Notes

1. Container traffic is measured in TEUs (twenty equivalent units) with one TEU being equal to one 20-foot-long container. The standard containers that make up the majority of international traffic are 10 feet wide and 10 feet high and are converted into TEUs in relation to their length. Thus a 40-foot-long container is equal to two TEUs, and a 10-foot-long container is 0.5 TEU.

4

A User's Manual for Italy

Alfonso Desiderio

Italy's extraordinary cultural and artistic heritage is a two-edged sword. It can come back to haunt Italians in an image of Italy as a nice place to visit but one of little consequence, or it can enhance Italy's influence throughout the world.

Can the world's greatest artistic heritage be an instrument of foreign policy like oil or the nuclear bomb, or could it become one?

This is a disconcerting question for many experts. For many years in Italy, cultural assets were looked on as a perpetual annuity that could be left alone, until it was discovered that they were an excellent source of money and jobs. Now they are being thought of as a geopolitical tool! Is it right to view culture as a tool? On second thought, the question first posed is not as simple as it seems.

On a trip to Damascus, Professor Paolo Matthiae recalled something Giulio Andreotti said while serving on the Foreign Affairs Committee of the Chamber of Deputies, on a break from the many government posts he has held. Professor Matthiae is the Italian archeologist whose discovery of the ancient city and civilization of Ebla was the culmination of the most extensive archeological undertaking since the period immediately following World War II. Andreotti's comment was, "Our country has limited foreign policy resources. We are not a superpower. We have an enormous wealth of cultural assets to draw upon, however, but we make very little use of them." But nothing much came of it, Matthiae noted.

Andreotti's generalization is even truer today. The players are country-systems, which amount to more than just the sum of a government's policies and economics; rather, they incorporate a number of different power factors. Each country has its unique strengths and must make the most of them to ensure that its country-system is competitive. The same holds true of enhancing a country's image. Italian negotiators working in the context of the European Union know something about this. Over and above the Maastricht requirements, they have to deal with anti-Italy and anti-Italian prejudices, which are widespread in Europe (as reflected by political leaders), or, on the other side of the coin, with Italian manufacturers who play up "Italian style" in order to place their products on worldwide markets. In this sense, artistic heritage is a geopolitical tool.

A Treasure Trove of Cultural Assets

Three thousand years of history, empires, invasions, and periods of great wealth and artistic sensitivity during which Italy was a political, economic, and religious center have made the Italian peninsula a treasure trove of cultural assets. Our artistic heritage is so great that we have not yet succeeded in cataloguing it; but our failure to preserve it has been equally great. We ourselves do not even know how many treasures we have. There are collections of data and partial estimates, however, that give us some idea: more than 2,000 archeological sites; some 20,000 historic town centers, from Rome to the Apennine mountain villages, with about a thousand in excellent condition; 40,000 fortresses and castles; 95,000 churches, a third with an important, often key, place, in art history; 1,500 monasteries; 30,000 historic residences with at least 4,000 gardens; thousands of historic libraries (3,100 of which are owned by the Catholic Church); more than 30,000 archives and, finally, more than 3,500 museums and galleries with their paintings and sculptures, not to mention works of art in foreign museums or private collections in Italy and abroad, legitimately or otherwise.[1]

In spite of this artistic inheritance—not to mention natural beauty, coasts, mountains, and an enviable climate—Italy ranked only fourth in the world in arrivals by foreign tourists for 1996 (according to World Tourism Organization statistics), behind France, the United States, and Spain. Italy welcomed 32.8 million foreign tourists, Spain 41 million, and France 61 million (double the number visiting Italy).

But that is not all. Up until the December 1997 session of the United Nations Educational, Scientific, and Cultural Organization (UNESCO), held in Naples, which marked a clear change of direction for the organization, the World Heritage List, compiled in accordance with the November 1972 Convention concerning the Protection of the World Cultural and Natural Heritage, included only 16 Italian "properties."[2] Italy ranked no higher than sixth, behind Spain (23), France (22), India (21), Germany (19), and the United States (18) and just ahead of China, Mexico, and Great Britain (16 each).[3] The ranking is tricky, of course, as sites are difficult to compare and many Italian historic centers contain dozens of works. But it is nevertheless hard to believe that young countries, culturally speaking, have more sites than Italy, not to mention Italy's loss of its seat on the executive board of UNESCO.

These are just a few of the symptoms of the marked lack of interest Italy has shown in its artistic heritage. The political stature of many ministers of cultural assets of the so-called First Republic and the short shrift given to art in Italian schools testify to the lack of interest in the country's artistic heritage at all levels. In the best Italian tradition, however, there has been no dearth of politicians, diplomats, and cultural figures who have launched praiseworthy initiatives. But they have almost always been isolated initiatives closely tied to the individual behind them, rather than a structured, organized policy designed to create a ripple effect in a country-system. But perhaps something is changing.

The Italian Renaissance

On the front page of the December 27, 1997, *International Herald Tribune*, the international daily newspaper of the European establishment, an article appeared under a telling headline: "In Italy, Signs of a Renaissance." The credit goes to Walter Veltroni, deputy prime minister and minister of cultural assets, who managed to complete projects that had been in the works for a long time and incorporate them into a more far-reaching policy that enabled him to bill the results as "events" to grab the attention of the Italian and foreign media. The article covered the December 16 opening of the archeological museum Palazzo Altemps, after 15 years of restoration. On opening day, the museum, just around the corner from Rome's Piazza Navona, whose collections include Greek and Roman sculpture, welcomed 27,000 visitors.

Table 4.1 1996 Attendance Figures and Revenues
(revenues in millions of U.S$)

Rank	Institution	Location	Total	Nonpaying	Paying	Revenues ($ millions)
1.	New and Old Archeological Areas	Pompeii (Naples)	1,906,337	555,487	1,350,850	10.51
2.	Uffizi Gallery and Vasarian Corridor	Florence	1,166,173	200,931	965,242	7.51
3.	Royal Palace and Park at Caserta	Caserta	1,025,167	566,225	458,942	1.66
4.	Palatine Hill and Forum of Rome	Rome	997,063	345,605	651,458	5.07
5.	Accademia Gallery	Florence	886,486	137,594	748,892	5.83
6.	Boboli Garden	Florence	816,495	218,207	598,288	1.55
7.	Villa d'Este	Tivoli (Rome)	543,086	172,701	370,385	1.92
8.	National Museum of Castel Sant'Angelo	Rome	434,455	117,255	317,200	1.65
9.	Flavian Amphitheater	Rome	420,071	137,648	282,423	1.46
10.	Palatine Gallery	Florence	412,911	94,223	318,688	2.48
11.	Medici Chapels	Florence	373,317	120,210	253,107	1.31
12.	Temples and National Museum at Paestum	Paestum (Salerno)	345,786	188,039	157,747	.82
13.	Accademia Gallery	Venice	310,213	70,913	239,300	1.86
14.	Villa Adriana	Tivoli (Rome)	301,130	125,220	175,910	.91
15.	Da Vinci's "The Last Supper"	Milan	292,812	23,690	269,122	2.09
16.	Museum of Egyptian Archeology	Turin	266,008	150,899	115,109	.89
17.	Archeological Area of Ostia Antica and Museum	Rome-Ostia	260,089	134,065	126,024	.65
18.	The Blue Grotto	Capri (Naples)	249,903	45,107	204,796	1.06
19.	National Archeological Museum	Naples	240,717	137,585	103,132	.80
20.	Borghese Gallery and Museum	Rome	163,094	44,742	118,352	.30
		Totals	11,411,313	3,586,346	7,824,967	50.33

Source: Ministry of Cultural Assets.   Note: 1,542.9 lire per U.S.$1 using 1996 exchange rate

Table 4.2   1997 Attendance Figures and Revenues
(revenues in millions of U.S.$)

Rank	Institution	Location	Total	Nonpaying	Paying	% Change 96-97	Revenues ($ millions)
1.	New and Old Archeological Areas	Pompeii (Naples)	1,964,279	576,919	1,387,360	3.04	9.78
2.	Uffizi Gallery and Vasarian Corridor	Florence	1,332,349	262,906	1,069,443	14.25	7.53
3.	Royal Palace and Park at Caserta	Caserta	1,076,550	629,469	447,081	5.01	1.49
4.	Palatine Hill and Forum of Rome	Rome	1,033,913	393,591	640,322	3.70	4.51
5.	Accademia Gallery	Florence	928,380	150,621	777,759	4.73	5.48
6.	Boboli Garden	Florence	886,077	259,505	626,572	8.52	1.47
7.	Flavian Amphitheater	Rome	660,671	217,607	443,064	57.28	2.24
8.	Villa d'Este	Tivoli (Rome)	574,816	203,214	371,602	5.84	1.74
9.	National Museum of Castel Sant'Angelo	Rome	533,900	114,600	419,300	22.89	1.97
10.	Palatine Gallery	Florence	411,748	104,679	307,069	-0.28	2.16
11.	Temples and National Museum at Paestum	Paestum (Salerno)	410,568	220,057	190,511	18.73	0.89
12.	Medici Chapels	Florence	403,359	140,217	263,142	8.05	1.24
13.	Villa Adriana	Tivoli (Rome)	315,131	140,427	174,704	4.65	0.82
14.	Accademia Gallery	Venice	314,604	84,104	230,500	1.42	1.63
15.	The Blue Grotto	Capri (Naples)	304,861	67,591	237,270	21.99	0.12
16.	Da Vinci's "The Last Supper"	Milan	302,636	17,330	285,306	3.36	2.00
17.	Museum of Egyptian Archeology	Turin	287,529	163,828	123,701	8.09	0.87
18.	Archeological Area of Ostia Antica and Museum	Rome-Ostia	279,164	162,418	116,746	7.33	0.55
19.	National Archeological Museum	Naples	258,301	153,336	104,965	7.30	0.74
20.	Borghese Gallery and Museum	Rome	247,824	85,750	162,074	51.95	0.98
	Totals		**12,526,660**	**4,148,169**	**8,378,491**	**9.77**	**49.23**

Source: Ministry of Cultural Assets.   Note: 1,703.1 lire per U.S.$1 using 1997 exchange rate

But other "signs of a renaissance" in Italian cultural policy after years of "indifference" did not escape the American journalist. Other accomplishments during Veltroni's nearly two years at the reins include the reopening of the Borghese Gallery after 14 years of restoration (with its sculptures by Bernini and paintings by Titian, Caravaggio, and Rafael, the museum brought in 220,000 visitors between July and December); the "Art under the Stars" initiative, which extended museum hours in the summertime; the Villa Borghese museum park in Rome; the addition of supplementary services at Italian museums, to exploit merchandising opportunities relating to Italian works of art and increase revenues; streamlining ticket sales; bringing in new financing with lottery drawings; and private investment incentives, such as the pilot project at Pompeii.

Even more interesting from a foreign policy standpoint is a new way of thinking on the part of the government, as noted by Armando Sanguini, director of the Office of Cultural Relations at the Ministry of Foreign Affairs. According to Sanguini,

> We have to think in terms of a country-system. Foreign Minister Dini has been pushing hard on this, and we are working toward that goal, as indicated most recently by the cultural component at "Vivere Italiano," the major exhibition opened by Dini and Minister Fantozzi. Another example is the agreement entered into with the Italian National Tourism Organization. We are also working with the Minister of Cultural Assets to make Cultural Assets Week an international event.

Veltroni echoed these comments at the UNESCO session held in Naples: "Efforts within Italy have also been broadened to the international arena, in an attempt to steadily increase awareness of the value of culture in the context of relations between and among governments, and with multilateral organizations and elsewhere."[4] The Naples session saw the addition of 10 new Italian sites to the list of World Heritage Sites marked for preservation, giving Italy 26 sites (plus one) out of a total of 552. In spite of its failure to hold onto its seat on the Executive Board, Italy now shares the top spot with Spain in the rankings by country.

"Italy is highly thought of at UNESCO," Sanguini goes on,

> and losing its seat on the Executive Board will not keep it
> from playing an important role. Although our goal is to
> win back our seat on the Executive Board two years from
> now, we are well represented on the committees that are
> the backbone of the organization. Our relationship with
> UNESCO is a priority, and the success of the Naples meet-
> ing is the result of our policy, which views culture as a
> primary goal on the bilateral, European, and multilateral
> stage.

Archeological Excavations and Restoration

Italy has 90 archeological excavation and restoration projects in
foreign countries, concentrated primarily in the Mediterranean
basin and the Middle East (including 10 in Libya and 8 in Turkey
and Jordan), but also in Eastern Europe (Rumania, Russia, and
Hungary), Africa (Sudan, Tanzania, Ethiopia, and Eritrea), Asia
(India, Laos, Nepal, Pakistan, and Thailand) and the Americas
(Bolivia, Mexico, and Peru).[5] In addition to their basic cultural
function, these projects are, or can become, a valuable foreign
policy tool. Just to cite two examples among many, the Italian-
Iraqi Archeological Institute and the Italian-Iraqi Institute for the
Restoration of the Monuments at Baghdad were the only two
Western scientific organizations to remain in operation during
and after the Gulf War. Today they host the Italian diplomatic
presence in Iraq.[6] In another example, an Italian diplomat in Syria
told Professor Matthiae, the Italian archeologist: "Here the real
Italian ambassador is you."

Almost all these projects, however, are run on a shoestring
budget underwritten by the Ministry of Foreign Affairs and universities, through the efforts of individual archeologists and a
few enlightened diplomats. "There has always been a lack of
synergy between these projects and foreign policy, which Italy
has never succeeded in capitalizing on," charges Fabio Isman, a
writer for the editorial page of the Rome daily *Il Messaggero* and
an expert on cultural assets.

According to Professor Matthiae, past archeological work in
foreign countries took the form of isolated initiatives, rather

than an organized policy, with the exception of the National School in Athens and the work begun by Giuseppe Tucci and institutionalized in the Italian Institute for Africa and the Orient (ISIAO), formerly known as ISMEO. France's Archeological Excavations Commission at its Ministry of Foreign Affairs works with a targeted policy, but does so on a grand scale with a sizable budget. By contrast, Germany has a less targeted but equally well-organized policy with the Berlin Archeological Institute and its field offices worldwide and universities. But in Italy, Matthiae points out, without Rome's La Sapienza University and the far-sighted efforts of then-Rector Antonio Ruberti, many excavations in the Middle East would not have received steady funding over the years.

And yet, archeological excavations and foreign policy are interconnected in a variety of ways. According to the chairman of the Archeology Department at La Sapienza,

> In Syria we have benefited greatly from Italians' ability to connect on a personal level better than other Europeans, who may have more money. But Italian foreign policy clearly paved the way in Arab countries. Today the success of Ebla has had a great international impact, especially in the Arab world.[7]

In fact, the Palestinian authority has picked Italy to resume the excavations at Jericho. These excavations are very important from the archeological standpoint, given the significance of the site and the fact that the modern stratigraphic method was used there for the first time in the 1950s. But they are also important from the political standpoint, given how sensitive relations with the Palestinian authority are and how important ancient history is for Israeli-Palestinian relations. The project was awarded to Professor Matthiae's research team, rejecting English and American offers, precisely because of the credibility won as a result of the Ebla excavations.

"These excavations also raise our profile from the political standpoint," Matthiae says,

> but we have to press the advantage. Our heritage is rich, but intangible. The most important thing is for cultural

research to be independent. In principle, cultural assets should be given equal importance. There cannot be scales of values, since otherwise culture can be manipulated. Archeology is often used for political ends. For example, in the Maghreb France excavated Roman sites almost exclusively, to justify the western presence in those countries. Tunisia reacted by going after Phoenician relics. And we know how important a role historical memory plays in the Arab-Israeli conflict.

Which brings us to the problem of reconciling geopolitical interests with cultural interests. Armando Sanguini has a ready answer:

This government views culture as a key component of Italian foreign policy, but that does not mean subordinating it to the short-term national interest. We take a longer view. Good foreign policy must take the cultural dimension into account, without placing any restrictions on cultural activities, since policy benefits from culture's ability to project its value and promote dialogue and communication. That is one of its essential features.

Italian Deputy Minister of Foreign Affairs Patrizia Toia points out another link between culture and geopolitics, the importance of a cultural bridge in bringing civilizations together and preventing a clash.[8] Sanguini makes the point even more clearly: "Culture is a strong but silent vehicle of dialogue, and has a valuable contribution to make in a variety of situations. For example, by keeping the cultural dimension from being defined too narrowly, it can help prevent people from thinking in terms of a clash of cultures." Professor Matthiae agrees: "Politics and economics are at the root of a thousand problems dividing North from South throughout the world. But other issues, like unitary religious policy, have a cultural basis. Given the universal value of cultural heritage, relations in this area can have a positive impact on important international policy issues."

Restoration is another area in which Italy can draw on a great tradition that is well respected around the world. In 1995, the Chinese city of Xian (Shaanxi Province) saw the opening of

Figure 4.1

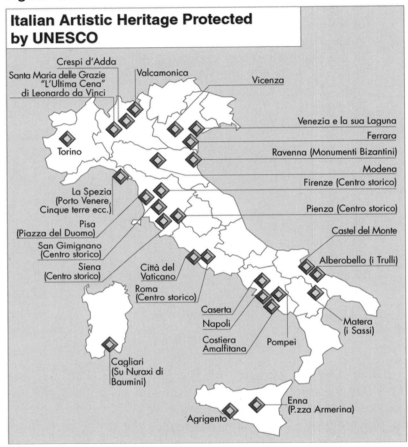

Key: "L'Ultima Cena"   "The Last Supper" (Leonardo da Vinci)
      Centro storico   Historic center
      Città del Vaticano   Vatican City
      Costiera Amalfitana   Amalfi Coast
      Monumenti Bizantini   Byzantine monuments
      Venezia e la sua laguna Venice and its lagoon

the Historical and Cultural Heritage Conservation and Restoration Training Center, serving all of Northwest China. The initiative is sponsored by ISIAO, the Ministry of Cultural Assets, the Central Restoration Institute, and the National Museum of Oriental Art. "Even though China has a high density of cultural assets and an established school of archeology," notes Roberto Ciarla, one of the leaders of the initiative,

> there was no national school of restoration that took a theoretical and methodological approach. After studying the American and English models, the Chinese selected the Italian school, now on the cutting edge through the efforts of [Directors] Argan and Brandi. The Xian Center was set up to train a new generation of specialized restorers using a multidisciplinary approach, and grew out of a joint effort by ISIAO and the Ministry of Foreign Affairs (the project was the brainchild of Ambassador Marco Francischi di Boschi).

China is the new frontier of cultural assets, with a great heritage that has not yet been brought to light or developed for tourism. But it will be, soon, as China's economic development and increasing openness to the West make a tourism boom a near certainty, so the competition is very tough. Ciarla continues:

> The Germans are very active in China. Although they are not much better funded, they have the advantage of a more established presence, more effective administration, and a more aggressive scholarship policy. By contrast, we fell three years behind during the rocky period for Italian foreign aid. [Editor's note: The Center project dates from 1992.] However, we are making progress and the school is doing very well. Some Chinese students traveled for four days to attend courses.

The complete lack of infrastructure in the Chinese cultural assets sector and the coming development boom should attract the attention of private-sector agencies and groups. "The only support we have received from the private sector, by contrast, is the offer by Banca Nazionale del Lavoro of airfare and a monthly stipend (1.5 million lire) for one of the Chinese scholarship recipients,"[9] notes Ciarla, who also serves as director of the archeological excavation project in Thailand, sponsored by ISIAO with minimal funding from the Ministry of Foreign Affairs and the Italian National Research Council (CNR).[10]

The Stele of Axum

In November 1997 during the first visit by an Italian president to Ethiopia, Oscar Luigi Scalfaro announced that the obelisk of Axum would be returned, another example of works of art being used as tools of foreign policy. The obelisk was carried off in 1935 as war booty and since then has remained on display in Rome in front of the FAO headquarters building, formerly the Ministry of Italian Africa. "The return of the stele of Axum," according to Minister Sanguini, "is a symbolic gesture that goes beyond the return of the object itself. It is an important sign that any shadow of the past has been overcome."

The return of the stele of Axum is not entirely unprecedented. Italy has returned other works of art in the past, such as the "Lion of Judah" to Ethiopia and the "Goddess of Butrinto" to Albania. Even so, a former occupying country returning the spoils of war is not an everyday occurrence.[11]

Italy itself was despoiled of more than one work of art during World War II. The Italian diplomat Rodolfo Siviero has long been a "hunter" of plundered Italian treasures,[12] especially those carried off by the Nazis toward the end of the war. Italy had always taken an extremely cautious stance on this subject until 1995, when, with the well-timed publication of the catalogue of 2,000 stolen Italian works of art[13] and the establishment of a special commission chaired by Ambassador Mario Bondioli Osio (still in existence today), then-Minister of Foreign Affairs Susanna Agnelli announced that the Italian government would do everything in its power to recover stolen works.[14]

The recovery of works of art stolen in wartime is a touchy subject in international relations, and it is complicated by the fact that all trace of many works has been lost and that others have been sold over time to various buyers. Moreover, if the rule were applied uniformly, many museums would lose their most prized collections. Armando Sanguini explains Italy's current position as follows: "Today we are working to make the return of works of art a point of agreement, rather than contention, while maintaining the principle that the claim for restitution of the work is valid."

But another feature of this issue should not be overlooked, and that is that the exhibition of Italian works of art abroad is an

An Artistic and Cultural Weapon

"At times we've felt like Don Quixote tilting at windmills," says General Roberto Conforti, head of the National Police unit responsible for the protection of artistic heritage since 1991, referring to Italians' marked lack of interest in cultural assets. "But things are different today," he goes on. "There is a new awareness and interest in seeing this sector take off."

Internationally, the National Police unit for the protection of artistic heritage is a feather in Italy's cap. This one-of-a-kind agency—France has a similar one, but it is much smaller—maintains a database of works of art stolen in Italy and abroad, which is considered the best in the world and makes significant monitoring possible. Established in 1969 on the foundation laid by the commission headed by Rodolfo Siviero, the diplomat who labored long to repatriate cultural assets carried off during World War II, the unit is responsible for protecting cultural assets and, especially, recovering stolen or illegally exported works of art, as well as regulating archeological sites. Although it operates under the direction of the Ministry of Cultural Assets, the unit maintains close ties to other law enforcement agencies, government offices, INTERPOL, the Ministry of Foreign Affairs, and Italian embassies.

"Italy is no shirk in how it manages its artistic heritage, as one would generally be led to believe," says General Conforti. "It is no accident that our legislation is cutting-edge." In 1997 nearly 2,000 thefts were reported in Italy (for a total of 23,000 artworks stolen), compared with more than 5,000 in France, not to mention Eastern European countries, where nothing short of plundering is under way.

The unit's international work is complicated by legislative differences and the sparse ratification of the applicable international conventions. But the recovery of the Capitoline Triad, illegally excavated near Guidonia and sold in Switzerland for 5 billion lire and about to be resold in the United States for 60 billion, is one of its major coups.

excellent way to promote Italy's image from the foreign policy standpoint. Even in faraway countries, people who have little chance to become acquainted with Italy through the media or in person are able to view Italian works of art and get a certain impression of Italy, almost like a permanent showroom abroad.

Geopolitical Tourism

"Tourism is, or can be used as, both an economic and political tool."[15] This statement by international tourism expert M. Crick is to be understood primarily in terms of a conception of tourism as a lockpick for gaining entry to closed political systems, like the former Soviet Union. Consider the importance given to tourism in the final act of the Helsinki Conference, or China, where Deng Xiaoping's economic revolution was accompanied by opening the country up to tourism. But D. L. Edgell's analysis goes even further: "The ultimate goal of political tourism is to integrate the economic, political, cultural, and intellectual benefits of tourism in an effort to improve overall quality of life and preserve peace and prosperity."[16] Examples include the integrating effect of tourism in Europe, especially by young people; Japan's policy of using tourism to partially compensate for its trade surplus and pursue other geopolitical goals;[17] or the use of tourism to bolster territorial claims.[18] But the importance "from the political standpoint of a host country using tourism to promote a specific image of itself throughout the world"[19] does not escape these scholars.

Of course, Italy has a great tradition of tourism. "Only in Rome have I discovered what it truly means to be human."[20] In a way, Goethe's famous words epitomize the eighteenth-century Grand Tour, when Europe's elite considered visiting Italy's cultural and natural beauties an indispensable part of their education. Today, cultural tourism is a mass phenomenon. In Italy, tourism in art centers accounts for 58 percent of the country's entire tourism market.[21] But for geopolitical purposes, the ability to communicate a specific image of Italy is just as important as the numbers. Italy cannot limit itself, as it did at the time of the Grand Tour and to some extent still does today, to exhibiting its cultural assets divorced from the political, economic, and social context that created them, preserved them and exhibited them.

The Italy visited in the eighteenth century by Europe's aristocrats and rich was devoid of Italians. The cultural treasures were looked on as an absolute value, independent of the Italians' handling of them, which was often criticized. By the same token, tourism today can be a two-edged sword, communicating an image of Italy as a nice place to visit, period; or even opening it up to criticism as works of art are destroyed, collapse, or fall into ruin.

Notes

1. See "Un Patrimonio di Tremila Anni" (Three thousand years of heritage), White Paper, Touring Club Italiano.

2. To which the Historic Center of Rome, which it shares with Vatican City, should be added.

3. A site in the Pyrenees shared by Spain and France should be added to the number for those two countries.

4. Speech given by Minister of Cultural and Environmental Assets Walter Veltroni at the Twenty-first Session of the UNESCO World Heritage Committee held in Naples, December 1, 1997. Press Office of the Ministry of Cultural Assets.

5. Ministry of Foreign Affairs, Missioni Archaeologiche Italiane (Italian Archeological Excavation Projects), "L'Erma" di Bretschneider, 1997.

6. Giorgio Gullini, Paper presented at the Meeting of Foreign Ministers on Italian Archeological Excavation Projects.

7. Probably more so than in Italy. In spite of the success of the 1995 exhibition on Ebla in Rome and Trieste, which was attended by 250,000 people, Matthiae has never been invited to speak to the Accademia Nazionale dei Lincei (Italian Academy of Sciences), whereas he has spoken to the Paris Academy on 15 occasions, twice to the London Academy, and at countless universities worldwide.

8. Meeting of Foreign Ministers on Italian Archeological Excavation Projects, January 22, 1998.

9. Unlike the domestic cultural assets sector, where progress is being made with private companies, the situation outside Italy is discouraging. Even Professor Matthiae admits that, in spite of the great impact the discovery of Ebla has had in Arab countries, private companies have never shown interest in the project.

10. Interestingly, unbeknownst to many in Italy, Italian culture has been a very important point of reference in Thailand for many years.

11. F. Isman, "L'Italia Restituice all'Etiopia l'Obelisco di Axum (Italy to return obelisk of Axum to Ethiopia)," *Il Messaggero,* November 25, 1997.

12. Ibid. In the 1960s, Siviero succeeded in recovering a number of masterpieces, such as the Ephebus of Selinunte.

13. Siviero had compiled the catalogue before then, but it had never been published for "diplomatic" reasons.

14. F. Isman, "La Agnelli: 'L'Italia Darà Battaglia per Riavere i Tesori Rubati in Guerra' (Susanna Agnelli: 'Italy will fight to recover treasures stolen in wartime')," *Il Messaggero,* October 11, 1995.

15. M. Crick, "Representations of International Tourism in the Social Sciences," *Annual Review of Anthropology,* 1989.

16. D. L. Edgell, *International Tourism Policy,* New York 1990, Van Nostrand Reinhold.

17. C. M. Hall, *Tourism and Politics,* Chichester 1994, Wiley.

18. This is true of territorial claims in the Arctic, the Antarctic, and the Spratley Islands in the South China Sea. These islands are uninhabited but hotly disputed by countries in the region for strategic reasons. Malaysia uses tourism to strengthen its claims.

19. C. M. Hall, *Tourism and Politics.*

20. "Ich kann sagen, daß ich nur in Rom empfunden habe, was eigentlich ein Mensch sei." J. W. von Goethe, *Reisen in Italien* (Travels in Italy).

21. Source: Ministry of Cultural and Environmental Assets.

5

From "Made in Italy" to *Sistema Italia:* In Search of an Internationalization Strategy

Marta Dassù and Roberto Menotti

In EURO-land, competition among country systems is ever fiercer. Is Italy ready to take up the challenge and project an organized system abroad? Are the Euro-Mediterranean scope of our geopolitics and the trend toward globalization in our economy in irreconcilable contradiction?

Is there any such thing as *Sistema Italia*? Stated another way, are the various Italian players on the international stage really perceived abroad as organized enough to be called a system?

Probably not. But there is no denying that projecting *Sistema Italia* abroad has become a kind of watchword in Italian foreign economic policy. Just consider the November 1997 initiative organized by Italy's Institute for Foreign Trade (ICE), a state agency, in Beijing in an undisguised effort to showcase *Sistema Italia* and reintroduce it into the most important emerging market, where Italy's commercial presence has been on the decline for several years. Or the Prodi and D'Alema governments' plans to promote *Sistema Italia*'s strengths on an international scale by talking up small and medium-sized enterprises and the industrial district model, especially in a forum like the Group of Seven (G-7). A document containing the 1999 policy guidelines issued by the Ministry for Foreign Trade in March is titled precisely "The Internationalization of *Sistema Italia*."[1] The document signals a determined effort to overcome a number of well-known deficiencies, as we will see in more detail in our concluding remarks.

In recent years, almost all of Italy's energy has been devoted to the primary goal of inclusion in the euro. Clearly, if Italy had not been accepted into the exclusive single-currency club after trying so hard to get in, *Sistema Italia* would have been discredited right from the start. Italy could then have retaliated by playing the "global pirate," as France accused it of doing in 1992, when it was excluded from the European monetary system. But the fate of Italy's economy and *Sistema Italia*'s reputation were unlikely to be gambled on a ploy as shortsighted (and misused, as the implications of the Asian financial crisis indicate) as a competitive devaluation race.

Because the real competition in the post–Cold War world is among efficient country-systems, and because Italy is off to somewhat of a late start in this regard (the overused expression "*Sistema Italia*" is a misnomer that underscores this lag), Italy's internationalization strategy is up against a number of obstacles, including tough choices in setting priorities.[2] Looking specifically at the relationship between foreign policy and foreign economic policy, the choices that the "systemic" approach call for do not seem so easy to boil down for Italy. Italy has strong regional interests (staying on the A-list of the European Union, or EU) and global trade interests but decidedly limited institutional resources and tools.

The Shopping List

Priorities have yet to be set, and so the task of bridging the gap between goals and how to achieve them remains undone. Every official foreign policy speech starts off deliberately enough, with the high priority of Europe. The speeches then unfailingly snowball to take in the Balkans, Italy's "Mediterranean prospects," the core importance of the "Atlantic Alliance," and Italy's unrelinquishable role as a "bridge" to Moscow. Then things really take off. . . . "And how could we forget Italy's global economic ambitions, as a country historically projected toward Asian markets and interested, for obvious reasons, in renewed relations with Latin America?" "And, of course, let us not overlook the vital importance for Italy of Africa's problems. We do not want to limit ourselves to failed efforts in Somalia or settle for Mozambique." Italy is at large in the world again.

In his June 1997 speech taking stock of a year of Italian foreign policy, Prime Minister Romano Prodi really did make an effort to be much more selective.[3] Nevertheless, the questions from the audience immediately found fault. ("Had he forgotten about

Argentina?" "Why had he not mentioned the North versus South problem?") The idea of foreign policy as an endless "shopping list" is hard to kill, even among Italians. We are too used to combining a pervasive lack of interest in international events with a very keen but sporadic interest in the most disparate of causes. Thus, the fate of Chiapas became more enthralling than the events in Albania. The mass media and general public apparently moved on, once the Alba mission was recalled.

These universalizing impulses are held in check by very limited tools, however. This discrepancy has always hurt the credibility of Italian foreign policy.

If we look at the tools first, rather than geographical priorities, Italy's sphere of influence immediately appears to contract sharply. Examples include the defense sector, in which the long, drawn-out affair of the new "model" finally resulted in a partial restructuring dominated by financial constraints; the drastic downsizing of aid to developing countries; or the difficult position the Ministry of Foreign Affairs finds itself in, as a combined result of one of the smallest budgets in Western Europe and prolonged stalling on internal restructuring. As with the Ministry of Defense, the outcome is a hybrid solution built around the addition of geographic coordination officers to the traditional subject-matter desks.[4]

Another example could be the unknown effect the proposed constitutional amendment passed by Parliament would have on the foreign policy decisionmaking process. The amendment calls for the creation of a Supreme Foreign Policy and Defense Council chaired by the directly elected president of the Republic. The entire scope of the Council's authority would be established by an act of Parliament. Obviously, if the Council were any more than a paper tiger (like the current Defense Council), there would be considerable danger of conflict between the Office of the President and the ministry, with their overlapping jurisdictions.

In short, a quick glance in Italy's toolbox—and one of the items in there should be reform of the Institute for Foreign Trade, a state agency—tells us two basic things right away. First, the resource problem is of prime importance (in a negative sense). Second, in an effort to cushion the impact of this shortage of resources, one of the root problems also relates to rethinking the relationship between the various levels on which,

Figure 5.1

The Fiat Group around the World

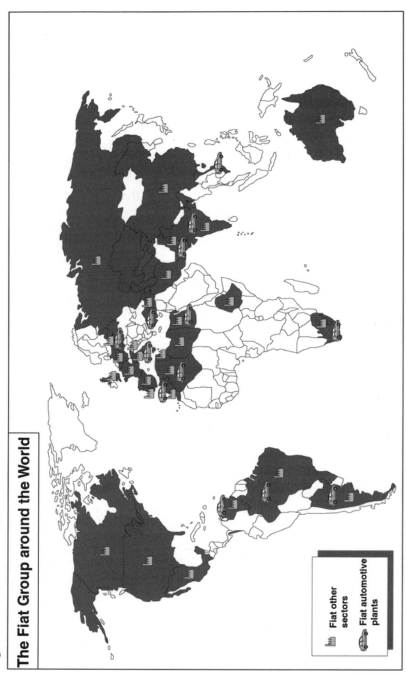

Fiat other sectors

Fiat automotive plants

and channels through which, Italy operates abroad (bilateralism and multilateralism, regionalism and globalism, nongovernmental policy and action taken by the government).

A Snapshot of Current Data

A snapshot of current conditions is a good place to start. What kind of influence does the "real-world Italy" have, and how much?

The data gathered by the authors on Italy's economic and commercial influence are certainly not original, but they are read in an unusual way to help redefine Italian policy priorities. As we just saw, this kind of undertaking is far from simple or automatic, but it could help close the gap between stated goals and the tools chosen to accomplish them.

A general idea of *Sistema Italia*'s standing in the international arena can be gleaned from some general data that provide points of reference. According to World Bank statistics, in 1995 Italy ranked sixth in gross national product (GNP), with approximately 4 percent of the world total.[5] It ranked sixteenth in per capita GNP, by contrast, with $19,020 in 1995 (ranking ahead of only Great Britain among G-7 countries); Italy recorded an average annual growth rate of 1.8 percent from 1985 to 1995, behind six of the countries that rank ahead of it in terms of per capita GNP.

Italy ranked thirty-ninth in economic competitiveness (according to World Economic Forum/Heritage Foundation estimates for 1995) and thirty-sixth in terms of "economic freedom" (well behind all five countries that rank ahead of it in terms of GNP).[6]

According to a study published in the weekly *Il Mondo* in mid-1997,[7] while Italy accounted for approximately 5 percent of world production, it represented only 1.5 percent of the "command capital" on the world market economy, such is the weight of the largest companies on the stock exchange value of the world's top 1,000 listed companies. Another point of concern is the trend from 1996 to 1997 in which French and British companies held fairly strong (although slipping a little), and Germany in particular made substantial gains (with seven new companies in the top 1,000 and a number of longtime leading companies moving up in the rankings). By contrast, Italy lost four spots in the top 1,000 (dropping from 17 to 13) and made an especially weak showing in the banking sector.

This is even more serious, considering the importance of the banking sector in a strategy to internationalize *Sistema Italia*.[8]

As a member of the International Monetary Fund or IMF (the organization with primary responsibility for monitoring and managing the international monetary system), Italy is required to pay a "fund quota" calculated by the IMF on the basis of the size of each country's economy, as well as its overall performance. Thus, while Germany and Japan have a quota of 5.67 percent, and France and the United Kingdom 5.10 percent, Italy is assigned a quota of 3.16 percent. As a result, by operation of an automatic mechanism Italy also wields a smaller percentage of total votes (i.e., less voting power) than those countries, with 3.09 (versus 5.54 for Germany and Japan and 4.98 percent for France and the UK).[9]

For Italy, foreign trade as a percentage of GDP was 47 percent in 1980 and 49 percent in 1995 (versus 24 percent for the United States, 17 percent for Japan, 46 percent for Germany, 43 percent for France, and 57 percent for Great Britain).[10] Clearly, the Italian economy is very exposed internationally.

In regard to outflows of direct foreign investment from Italy, there is a marked imbalance between Italy's GDP rank (sixth in the world) and its relative weight as an international investor (sixteenth in the world). Italy accounted for 3.2 percent of European Executive Entrepreneurs worldwide in 1995, substantially lower than its share of worldwide exports (4.6 percent). This same disinclination against direct investment makes Italy's commercial presence in emerging markets fragile by definition. (Significantly, Italy's position as China's second-leading West European trading partner has been gradually eroded during the 1990s.)

The picture presented in tables 5.1 and 5.2 takes on special significance in relation to the substantial change over the last ten years in terms of the internationalization of Italian industry. The positive balance shown in the data snapshot of what the tables' authors call "multinational flight"—the fact that there are more Italians working abroad in companies directly held by Italian investors than employees of foreign holdings in Italy—is something new that would have been unthinkable only ten years ago. Evalu-

Table 5.1   Italian Industry Abroad (1995 data)

Industrial companies abroad in which Italian investors hold a stake	1,842
Italian investors abroad (groups and companies)	622
Total personnel abroad	**595,547**

Source: R. Cominotti, S. Mariotti, *Italia Multinazionale 1996*, Milan 1997, Franco Angeli.

Table 5.2   Foreign Holdings of Italian Industry (1995 data)

Italian industrial companies in which foreign investors hold a stake	1,630
Foreign investors in Italy (groups and companies)	966
Total foreign personnel in Italy	**527,461**

Source: R. Cominotti, S. Mariotti, *Italia Multinazionale 1996*, Milan 1997, Franco Angeli.

ating this piece of information in strategic terms, however, foreign holdings in Italy are different in kind from Italian holdings abroad. The Italian presence is polarized toward countries with productive functions and labor-intensive technologies (requiring a large labor force), while foreign holdings in Italy are capital-intensive and much larger in terms of sales. Looking solely at controlling interests, the ratio of inflows to outflows is very high.

During the 1980s, the principal players of internationalization (within the ambivalent and piecemeal Italian framework) were large industrial companies. In the 1990s, once the initial groundbreaking rush had tapered off, small and medium-sized enterprises (SMEs) led the way and left their mark of broader and deeper penetration abroad, confirming that the process was reaching maturity.

SMEs play a leading role in Italian exports. A 1995 survey found that foreign countries were the pivotal market for no less than 31 percent of businesses operating in industrial districts, versus 18 percent for all businesses.[11] Stated another way, industrial districts are particularly dependent on foreign markets. Further

Table 5.3   Italian Overseas Development Assistance, 1995
(millions of 1995 U.S.$)

	Payments	Commitments
Bilateral	611	451
Multilateral, of which	794	793
voluntary contributions	132	131
mandatory contributions	79	79
share of EU aid	576	576
share of IIF assets	7	7
Total ODA	1,405	1,244

Source: Italian Ministry of Foreign Affairs, *Annual Report on Development Assistance Policy Implementation in 1995*, 1996.

Exchange rate: 1995 – 1,628.9 lire per U.S.$1

confirmation comes from the data on the value of exports from 1992 to 1996: the ten regions of Italy growing faster than the national average are weighted heavily toward northeastern and central Italy (with the exception of Lazio). Production in these regions typically centers around SMEs, which are often geographically integrated on the industrial district model.[12]

The most recent data on direct foreign investment by Italy show a drop in the size of new ventures—confirming previous data—and substantial interest in developing areas feeling the pull of worldwide trends (Eastern Europe, Latin America, and the Pacific).

An important consequence of the small scale of direct foreign investment by Italy—which in some ways is cause for concern in the long run—relates to how the investment breaks down by sector. Using Pavitt's taxonomy, which provides a handy system of industrial classification,[13] the high-technology and specialized sectors are poorly represented. Underrepresentation in the high-tech sector is associated with the weakness of Italy's system of innovation and lack of Italian groups in the key electronics, electronic data communications and telecommunications, pharmaceuticals, and chemicals sectors. Underrepresentation in the specialized sector is associated with the difficulties faced by small and medium-sized enterprises in garnering substantial market power, regardless of how competitive they are from a qualitative standpoint.

This all points back to *Sistema Italia*'s inability to provide a favorable institutional environment.

**Table 5.4   Voluntary Contributions to Principal
International Organizations, 1995**
(billions of lire)

	1993	1994	1995
UNDP	40.0	40	30.0
United Nations Development Program			
UNICEF	38.2	29	20.0
United Nations Children's Fund			
UNDCP	26.0	20	14.0
United Nations International Drug Control Program			
FAO	28.8	25	20.0
Food and Agriculture Organization (UN)			
WHO	8.0	6	5.6
World Health Organization (UN)			
WFP	11.9	9	3.5
World Food Program (UN ECOSOC)			
UNHCR	16.0	16	12.0
United Nations High Commissioner for Refugees			
UNRWA	15.0	15	12.0
United Nations Relief and Works Agency for Palestine Refugees in the Near East			

Source: Italian Ministry of Foreign Affairs, *Annual Report on Development Assistance Policy Implementation in 1995,* 1996.

Exchange rates: 1993 – 1,573.7 lire per U.S.$1; 1994 – 1,612.4 lire per U.S.$1; 1995 – 1,628.9 lire per U.S.$1.

In a nutshell, Italian companies, even though they have grown rapidly since the 1980s, still are not international enough to meet the challenges of global competition, despite the clear competitive advantages the medium-sized ones enjoy.[14] Only the companies themselves can make the qualitative leap. A more favorable institutional environment is also needed. But more urgent choices absolutely must be made first, and other conditions must be satisfied (developing the banking system, coordination efforts, and so forth).

Partners Near and Far

Even a cursory review of commerce data reveals that industrialized nations are well represented among Italy's trading partners. Considering the top priority given to the competitiveness of exports, this feature calls for close attention.

The top 20 non-EU countries to which Italy exports include Japan, Hong Kong, Turkey, Russia, Poland, Brazil, China, and South Korea (1995 data). Interestingly, the list is almost exactly the same for imports, with the exception of Libya at number 15 for obvious reasons relating to energy needs.

The preeminence of Germany and France among Italy's trading partners, followed by the United States and Great Britain, points to the fact that the "hard core" of Italy's international presence still centers around its tried and true partners. Geopolitical and geoeconomic propensity coincide in this case, therefore, giving rise to the primacy of the European "circle" in Italian foreign policy. Essentially, Italy has stepped up its presence in markets outside the European community during the 1990s,[15] but the overall picture still centers around its European partners and the United States.

Data on emerging markets reveal a sporadic interest in Latin America. A few countries with significant potential are becoming more important as channels of trade for Italian exports, but without specific, high-profile policy initiatives, while a more coordinated effort is being made to catch up in Asian markets.[16] In the Asian-Pacific region, foreign policy is now fairly avowedly in the service of Italy's economic presence. From Italy's viewpoint, the key countries in the region are India, China, and Japan (the effects of the 1997 crisis should confirm the dominance of India and China in Italian economic diplomacy, even if growth expectations are scaled back in the case of China and new unknowns are introduced).

There seems to be room on the African continent for a stepped-up Italian presence in sub-Saharan economies with significant development potential. But apart from a presence in a few very specific sectors (mining-extraction and infrastructure), it is hard to imagine that Italy can afford to expend any more energy there, given the difficulties it already has in maintaining a "critical mass" in other regions calling for its attention.

This is also true of an area that seems like Italy's home turf: the Mediterranean. Foreign trade data reveal a decline in relation to Italy's import and export quotas, compared with an increase in trade with Asia and, to a certain extent, Latin America. A lower rate of Italian investment is also being recorded in Mediterranean countries with respect to other regions. It would therefore

Figure 5.2

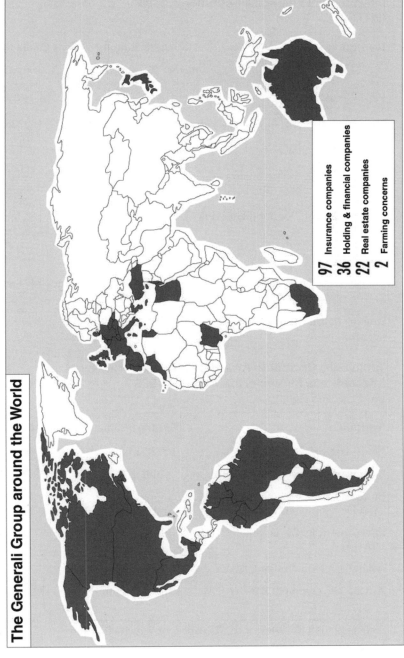

The Generali Group around the World

97 Insurance companies
36 Holding & financial companies
22 Real estate companies
2 Farming concerns

**Table 5.5   Italian Representation in
International Financial Institutions, 1996**
(in U.S.$ and ECU)

Institution	Italian Personnel		Italy's Quota Share	
	number	*% of total*	*%*	*amount*
World Bank	54	1.3	2.9	$4.480 million
International Monetary Fund (IMF)	53	2.3	3.16	$3.421 million
European Investment Bank (EIB)	160	17.0	17.5	65 billion ECU
European Bank for Reconstruction and Development (EBRD)	40	6.5	8.52	1.7 billion ECU
Inter-American Development Bank (IADB)	10	0.8	1.89	$1.328 million
Asian Development Bank (AsDB)	9	1.4	1.86	$405 million
African Development Bank (AfDB)	2	0.2	2.64	$474 million

Source: Italian Ministry of the Treasury, 1997 Annual Report.

**Table 5.6   Contracts Awarded to Italian Firms by
International Financial Institutions, 1996**
(in U.S.$ and ECU)

Institution	Contract Value	% of All Contracts
World Bank	$673.5 million	5.7
European Investment Bank (EIB)	4 billion ECU	17.0
European Bank for Reconstruction and Development (EBRD)	175 million ECU	10.2
Inter-American Development Bank (IADB)	$110 million	2.6
Asian Development Bank (AsDB)	$210 million	5.7
African Development Bank (AfDB)	$139.9 million	8.5

Source: Italian Ministry of the Treasury, 1997 Annual Report.

appear to be the case that, if current trends continue, the Mediterranean will be largely relegated to the energy sector in terms of the Italian economic presence.

Words of Caution

As this picture develops, more thorough assessments of how the government can support the internationalization of the Italian economy—i.e., what the relationship is between the real-world Italy and Italy as it exists on paper—are beginning to take shape.[17] Significantly, the most recent ICE report offers a specific word of caution on the trade balance issue, when it asserts that

> progress in trade . . . must not be mythologized in a quasi-commercialistic sense, but seized on as an opportunity to impel the system of production toward broader internationalization strategies: stable commercial penetration efforts, brand-name and merchandising policies, customer service, direct foreign investment (as majority investors or through joint-ventures), technology transfer agreements, industrial collaboration and technical assistance in broad segments of the industrial and agricultural sectors in developing countries.

Stated another way, while it is true that the flexibility and adaptability of the Italian output structure should be viewed as a competitive advantage to be pressed as far as possible, it is equally true that continuity and a systematic approach (geographically and otherwise) in all efforts by the private sector and government institutions are necessary preconditions for the establishment of a solid economic presence in the most promising markets. As the ICE report goes on to argue, while planning action to encourage companies to internationalize,

> the urge to raise Italian export quotas in all markets and growth sectors in which they are low must be resisted. . . . A country's comparative advantages (sectoral and geographic) must be weighed, and not brushed aside to chase after ups and downs in demand.

Another important observation in the ICE report relates to the advisability of some forms of corporate assistance. It can be read as an expression of uncertainty, rather than one lacking in discernment, as to how to the problem of international competitiveness is to be addressed and what the government's special role should be in promoting Italian businesses:

> It must first be said that, in today's environment with the system of multilateral rules on international trade gaining strength, the arguments of those who have long held that using public funds to provide corporate subsidies is ill-advised can no longer be ignored. It is not so much a fear that that the workings of markets would be distorted, although their oligopolistic structure would render them imperfect, as it is a matter of weighing the dangerous consequences if governments started competing to offer their businesses ever greater facilities.

> Stated another way, the decision to continue and even step up a given public assistance program should not be based solely on the argument that Italian corporations should not be placed at a disadvantage with respect to the competition. Specific arguments should be made for the advisability of a subsidy, failing which the best solution could be a concerted effort to convince the proper international organization to multilaterally scrap harmful, or even just superfluous, forms of assistance.

It will come as no surprise that the issue of the relationship between national policies and the workings of the international economy is extremely complex, especially in the face of "globalizing" trends, which are in turn triggering "localizing" reactions and even breakups. Nevertheless, the brief mention the report quoted above makes is indicative of the kind of problems that could arise. Although the report emphasizes that "these general observations do not do away with the need to make increasingly efficient and coordinated use of the tools a country chooses, to encourage its companies to internationalize," it warns against using them without a clear unifying vision and rigorous plan.

Figure 5.3

Olivetti around the World

Europa

Francia: Parigi
Spagna: Madrid e Barcellona
Portogallo: Lisbona
Belgio: Bruxelles
Olanda: Leiden
Germania: Norimberga e Francoforte
Austria: Vienna
Svizzera: Zurigo
R. Unito: Londra e Milton Keynes
Danimarca: Brondby
Finlandia: Helsinki

Norvegia: Oslo
Svezia: Stoccolma
F. Jugoslava: Belgrado
Slovenia: Koper
Cechia: Praga
Slovacchia: Bratislava
Ungheria: Budapest
Polonia: Varsavia
Estonia: Tallin
Romania: Bucarest
Cgi: Mosca
Grecia: Atene

Asia

Cina: Pechino
Giappone: Tokio
Corea: Seul
Malesia: Kuala Lumpur
Filippine: Merkaty City
Singapore
Hong Kong
Thailandia: Bangkok
Vietnam: Hanoi
Israele: Herzilya Pituash
Iran: presente attraverso agenti
Siria:
Arabia Saudita:
Oman:
Yemen:
Kuwait:
Libano:

Africa

Sud Africa: Johannesburg e Paulshof
Algeria: Presente attraverso agenti
Marocco:
Tunisia:
Egitto:
Eritrea:
Etiopia:
Capo Verde:
Nigeria:
Costa d'Avorio:
Kenya:
Senegal:
Seychelles:
Tanzania:

Oceania

Australia: Silverwater

Nord America

Canada: Toronto
Usa: Bridgewater, New York e Liberty Lake WA
Messico: Atzacapotzalco

America Latina

Argentina: Buenos Aires
Cile: Santiago
Brasile: San Paolo
Perù: Lima
Colombia: Bogotà
Venezuela: Caracas
Puerto Rico

The goal of consolidating and establishing an economic presence abroad calls for great discernment in identifying the countries and sectors in which that effort is farsighted, profitable, and, of course, feasible.

The 1997 annual report of the Italian Ministry of the Treasury, which deals with 1996 data, offers another view. From 1986 to 1996 Italy earmarked 700 billion lire annually to fund international financial institutions operating in developing and transitioning countries. The report states that Italian commitments totaled 1.164 billion lire in 1996 and adds that the percentage of Italians working at these institutions is ridiculously low, especially when talking about high-level posts (see table 5.5).

This confirms Italy's image as a politically underrepresented country, due to the lack of powerful business interests to back Italian candidatures from the Ministries of the Treasury and Foreign Affairs and from the Bank of Italy. As Enzo Quattrociocche, director for Italy of the European Bank for Reconstruction and Development, said recently,[18] the lack of strategic planning in the management of candidatures for international positions, which correlates to a culture of emergence in relation to international events, and the lack of international prospects have stood in the way of a country plan and a human resources development strategy.

Italy is underrepresented, then, not just in relation to its political standing as a G-7 country, its level of contribution to individual institutions, and its economy's influence in the international community, but in relation to its actual rank in terms of the development banks' own procurement data (based on contracts awarded to Italian firms for construction, supplies, and services, as the result of an international competitive bidding process, and its participation in private projects as a donor).[19]

Regionalism and Globalism

Political and security needs are also taken into consideration in government policy decisions to back international economic efforts. The interaction between the data discussed above and Italian foreign policy offers an insight into how "coherent" Italy's international influence is.

Looking at Italian foreign policy in the 1990s, there are two very general themes that carry over from the postwar tradition.[20]

The first is Italy's stated desire to hold onto its place among the nucleus of advanced nations and not be excluded from decisionmaking forums. This desire applies to the euro and the Security Council, and received a painful rebuke in the affair of the Contact Group on Bosnia. This insistence on being "in" has matured since the 1947 Peace Treaty and shown itself on several occasions since then. The great departure from the past is that, if Italy wants to continue to "participate," it must assume costs, responsibilities, and direct obligations. Status (or rank) and role have become interdependent, now that the automatic workings of the Cold War no longer apply.

The second carryover is the strategy of using an outside obligation for domestic administrative purposes, a strategy explicitly adopted with the Tax for Europe. Again in a departure from the past, the actual costs of such a strategy have become very high, but it continues to enjoy broad-based support within Italy. Periodic polls of European public opinion show that Italians are still substantially pro-Europe, unlike the Germans or French.

The predominance of these two factors, so central to Italian foreign policy, in fact puts the country in a very delicate position. Since Italy succeeded in joining the ranks of the euro while staving off unwanted reform of the Security Council, it has come away with a healthy dose of self-confidence. If this had not happened, the repercussions within Italy would have been staggering, especially in the case of the euro.

The perception that this is a difficult and risky situation is reinforced by the fact that, since the breakup of the blocs, Italy is more directly exposed to the instability of southeastern Europe and the Mediterranean (one need look no further than the impact of migration).

The most concerted efforts to promote stability while establishing an Italian presence seem to be directed toward the Balkans and Central and Eastern Europe as a whole. Active participation in the complicated processes of expanding the EU and NATO, subregional initiatives promoted by Italy, bilateral ties, and new foreign aid policy are all at work simultaneously in that area. Southeastern Europe is therefore a "high-density" area for Italy and will probably become even more so if political stability increases. In that region Italy has the special problem of avoiding a North/South "rift," especially in regard to politics and security (thus, Italy's repeated insistence on "balanced" NATO and EU expansions).

On the subject of stability in southeastern Europe, Italy has taken an important stand on Turkey, as a player in a key location for many Italian geopolitical and geoeconomic interests. A sign of the attention Italy is now paying to Turkey—which is having a profound influence on the development of another strategically important region, namely, Central Asia—came in December 1997 at the European Summit in Luxembourg, where the European Union made the decision not to include Turkey for now among the countries selected for admission or pre-admission talks. Italy criticized the decision openly, thereby departing somewhat from the position taken by its European partners. As the Italians saw it, facilitating Turkish participation in the European Conference[21] the following spring would have been a good idea.

From the political and economic standpoint, Italy sees the Mediterranean first and foremost in terms of the Euro-Mediterranean partnership (EU); second in terms of the embryonic multilateral cooperation among several European countries in the area of security and military alliance (the Western European Union, or WEU, and bilateral accords); and last, potentially, in terms of a greater role by NATO (possibly broadening the "Mediterranean dialogue" being carried on by NATO and the six countries along the southern coast that have been involved in the initiative so far). Economic and commercial interests seem to take a back seat to security concerns in this case or, at least, "economic security," concerns that essentially relate to energy imports (Italian dependence on imports from OPEC countries increased substantially from 1993 to 1996). The economic clout of the countries along the southern coast of the Mediterranean in respect to worldwide trade and growth still seems too limited for autonomous economic interests (the search for opportunities in various product sectors) to trigger an integrated response at the country-system level.

The Geopolitics of Foreign Aid

Development assistance is an area in which geopolitical interests now seem to take precedence over economic considerations. Now that the "commercial" phase of the last decade is over (with the Tangentopoli scandals[22]), development assistance has been drastically scaled back, and the new policy line seems inspired by a vision dominated by the goal of stability in "nearby foreign countries." Other goals are secondary, like enhancing historical ties with African partners and using foreign aid as a corporate assistance tool. At the same time, it is also clear that a focusing of aid (e.g., on a much smaller number of key countries in contrast to a tradition of "spreading it around") is also dictated by very tight budgetary constraints.

Another important factor is the choice of multilateral (or multibilateral[23]) assistance, which has now become fairly clear-cut. The main purpose is to consolidate Italy's "rank" in terms of multilateral commitments, but it is also an effect of the inhibitions done away with by the Tangentopoli experience. With the bilateral channel cut to the bone, there arises a certain preference for fund management by international organizations like the World Bank (as in the case of Albania, where Italy is the number-one donor).

Very briefly, for a long time Italy took a "global niche" approach to foreign aid, although there was a group of fairly stable, albeit diverse, recipients. Recently, a tendency toward "localism" has emerged, based on the principle of geographical contiguity (Bosnia, Albania). While the global niche approach reflected economic interests, political lobbies, and universalizing sociocultural pressures, the tendency toward localism reflects the idea that foreign policy and security are more closely intertwined, as well as the scarcity of available funds.

This kind of framework fails to take into account a case like the relationship with Mozambique, which was built on the success of nongovernmental mediation without any detailed geopolitical or geoeconomic assessment. To an extent, such relationships tend to develop out of an assistance policy involving a variety of private-sector players.

In Search of Style

Obviously, the geopolitical horizon is essentially regional for a country like Italy, and the data confirm this impression. That horizon is limited to Europe (now expanded to include the former Communist countries), with its Balkan and Mediterranean appendixes. Italy's geoeconomic prospects, on the other hand, are necessarily global, and this has political and security implications ranging from the protection of investments to Italy's aspirations for an international status commensurate with its role as a trading power. The divergence between Italy's geoeconomic and geopolitical prospects—and between the real-world Italy and Italy as it exists on paper—complicates thinking about Italian foreign policy and the projection of Italian influence abroad. The coherence one would expect to see between the current primary goal of Italian foreign policy (stable inclusion in a successful euro) and Italy's global ambitions as described above is, in fact, not there.

Things would be simpler if the EU actually became an autonomous, influential player on the international stage, as the functionalist outlook of those who expect political and diplomatic developments to come out of the introduction of the euro would have it. If that happened, the regionalist approach would also reinforce the tendency toward globalism. Although that is not guaranteed to happen, Italy will in any event have to face difficult challenges and make hard choices.

Of course, Italy will only manage to stay on its feet in the new global competition if (1) it manages to hold its strong regional nucleus together; (2) it succeeds in pushing its special interests through at the tough European bargaining table; and (3) it adapts its system to meet international challenges.

All this means—and this also goes for that part of the international system some academics call the postmodern world[24]—that the lines between domestic policy and foreign policy will get even blurrier; there will be an unprecedented degree of reciprocal interference and oversight in the traditional spheres of domestic policy (ranging from the convergence criteria to the intrusive powers of the World Trade Organization); relations among European countries will be built on an unstable mixture of extensive cooperation (including the relinquishment of sovereignty in some areas) and renewed competition. In theory, a country like Italy is more prepared than other countries to adapt to some of these post-bipolar restrictions precisely because of the evident weakness of its "national character." The other side of the coin is that Italy cannot project a coherent national policy abroad. All things considered, this is the source of the strengths and weaknesses of *Sistema Italia*. This is what makes the European option so attractive, and it is also the source of the relative "immaturity" with which Italy has long conceived its relationship with Europe.

Figure 5.4

Nuovo Pignone around the World

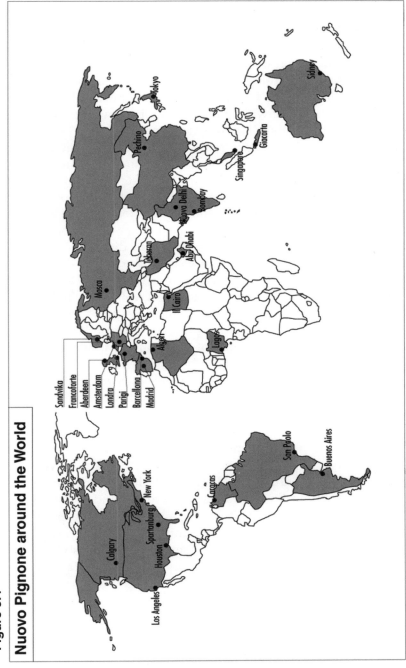

It will come as no surprise to anyone and has been touched on above, but perhaps it bears repeating in this connection that Italy's high degree of interdependence with the major industrialized nations, primarily Germany and France, is what mainly makes it stand out on the international economic stage. There is no need to stress the role those two countries will play in determining the direction the European Union and the single currency will take. Italy's future will be determined by how it participates in this difficult process of building Europe. That may be a banal statement, but its importance must not be underestimated.

The policy guideline for the year 1999 issued in March by the Ministry for Foreign Trade calls for a "systemic strategy" designed to further promote the internationalization of Italian firms. Specifically, a new interagency committee charged with coordinating Italy's trade policies is being established: this unit, also known as the *cabina di regia*–a film director's chair–for internationalization, is intended to serve as the hub of the institutional-productive system. This concerted effort should certainly be regarded as a positive sign. Italy is thus well aware that in the new framework of the euro the competitiveness of *Sistema Italia* is even more important than before, precisely because Italy remains essentially a latecomer in terms of rationalization of its external projection.

By virtue of its size, objective influence, and geopolitical position, Italy cannot be equated to the Netherlands and therefore cannot conduct its foreign policy along similar lines (in the tradition of a merchant country closely linked to German hegemony). Given its tradition and "national character" (i.e., the expression of the society and its institutions over time), it is not even the equivalent of a small France (a country with a tradition of national power within Europe). It must therefore find its own individual style of projecting its influence abroad, once the era of the postwar style (big decisions on alignment, and keeping a low profile) has passed by definition. Then, even if that style is not exactly the "Made in Italy" style promoted by Italian fashion designers, *Sistema Italia* will have made some progress.

Notes

1. Ministero del Commercio con l'Estero (Ministry for Foreign Trade), *L'internazionalizzazione del Sistema Italia, Linee direttive programmatiche 1999* (The internationalization of sistema Italia), March 1999. Rome.

2. For a comprehensive discussion of this topic, see G. Bonvicini and P. Guerrieri Paleotti, eds., *Per una politica economica estera dell'Italia nell'era della competizione globale* (Toward a foreign economic policy for Italy in the era of global competition), December 1997, Institute of International Affairs (IAI), Mediocredito Centrale.

3. "Un anno di politica estera" (A year of foreign policy), speech given by Prime Minister Romano Prodi to the Italian Center for Studies in International Conciliation, Rome, July 16, 1997, Banca di Roma, Palazzo de Carolis.

4. See the speech given by Foreign Minister Dini to the Senate Foreign Affairs Committee on the ministry's budget, October 21, 1997. The foreign minister has set up forums and regional roundtables to facilitate periodic meetings between institutions and the business community, another step in the direction of *Sistema Italia*, according to Dini (L. Dini, "Globalizzazione: l'Italia accetta la sfida. Questo è il nostro impegno" (Italy accepts the challenge of globalization. That is our pledge), *Telèma,* Winter 1997–1998).

5. World Bank, *The State in a Changing World, World Development Report 1997,* New York 1997, Oxford University Press.

6. The United States ranked third and fifth, respectively; Japan, fourteenth and eleventh; Germany, twenty-fifth and twentieth; France, twenty-third and thirty-first (the only indicator in the same ballpark as the one for Italy); and Great Britain, seventh and seventh.

7. *Il Mondo,* July 12, 1997, pp. 3, 14–27.

8. A uniquely Italian paradox can be found in the effort to base the internationalization of trade on the rapid growth of small and medium-sized enterprises (SMEs), when they are penalized by an inflexible banking industry. There is a "supply relationship" model for a convenience good (funds) that puts small and medium-sized enterprises facing international competition at a competitive disadvantage. But encouraging signs are starting to be seen: Along with the restructuring of the banking system, companies are trying to bring their financial management and equity base up to date. See G. Forestieri, "I sistemi bancari tra ristrutturazione ed innovazione" (Banking systems between restructuring and innovation), *Studi e Note di Economia,* No. 3/1996, Banca del Monte dei Paschi di Siena.

9. Internet site of the International Monetary Fund. The United States has far and away the highest quota (18.25 percent) and percentage of votes (17.78 percent).

10. World Bank, *World Development Report 1997.*

11. Italian Central Bureau of Statistics (ISTAT), *Rapporto sull'Italia, Edizione 1997* (Italy report 1997), Bologna 1997, Il Mulino, p. 86.

12. Ibid., p. 85.

13. K. Pavitt, "Sectoral Patterns of Technical Change: Towards a Taxonomy and a Theory," *Research Policy,* Issue No. 13/1984.

14. See a summary of the At-Kearney Report on 65 medium-sized Italian companies in *Il Sole-24 Ore,* February 5, 1998, p. 3.

15. Italy's share of direct exports to the European Union fell from 61.5 percent to 55 percent from 1992 to 1996 (ICE Report 1996, pp. 29-30).

16. See J. L. Rhi-Sausi, ed., "La riscoperta dell'America Latina" (The rediscovery of Latin America); and M. Dassù, ed., "Per una strategia italiana verso la Cina. Il mito di Marco Polo alla prova" (Towards a China strategy for Italy: Testing the Marco Polo myth), International Policy Laboratory, 1997, Institute of International Affairs (IAI).

17. See L. Incisa di Camerana, "La posizione dell'Italia" (Italy's position), in ISPI, *1995-1996: La dis-unità del mondo* (1995-1996: World disunity), (Report on the state of the international system), Milan 1997, pp. 285–303.

18. *Il Sole-24 Ore,* January 26, 1998, p. 23.

19. The World Bank is a good example: 5.7 percent of all contracts financed by the Bank were awarded to Italians. This puts Italy first among industrialized countries in the contract value rankings, but the organization's staff currently includes only 54 Italians, none very high up (there are no Italian executives). Italians play a very limited role in consulting services, accounting for $4.1 million in 1996, or 0.28 percent of the value of the contracts awarded in the sector (0.2 percent for the African Development Bank). The language problem and the lack of international expertise seem to play a role in this area.

20. On these two points see also L. Incisa di Camerana, "La posizione dell'Italia" (Italy's position).

21. *Corriere della Sera,* December 16, 1997, p. 8, and December 17, 1997, p. 11.

22. Tangentopoli, which literally means "Kickback City," is a term used for the corruption scandals that came to light in the early 1990s. The scandals involved the highest levels of Italian government and industry.

23. The "multibilateral" channel means the management of Italian bilateral funds by multilateral organizations through cofinancing and fiduciary trusts.

24. See R. Cooper, *The Post-Modern World*, London 1996, Demos.